How To Survive Protracted Litigation

When the American Judicial System STOPPED Being Fair and Impartial

Claudia Barber

Kingdom Publishing, LLC, 1350 Blair Dr, Ste F, Odenton, MD 21113
First printed in the United States of America

Table of Contents

Dedication

This book is dedicated to my dearest parents, Elder Theodore L. Barber and Missionary Pauline Barber, and my siblings, Paul Barber and Marilyn Barber. It is also dedicated to many fearless social justice advocates like Carl Snowden, convener of the Caucus of African-American Leaders in Maryland, Judge Frederick K. Foote, Jr., and Reverend Stephen Tillett of the Anne Arundel County NAACP. I also treasure the love and support of my pastors: the late Apostle Leroy H. Cannady, Sr., Bishop James D. Nelson Sr., and Bishop Monroe Saunders, Jr.

Preface

James Baldwin once critiqued the United States criminal justice system (n.d.):

> If one really wishes to know how justice is administered in a country, one does not question the policemen, the lawyers, the judges, or the protected members of the middle class. One goes to the unprotected...and listens to their testimony.

These words resonate today. That is why I dedicate this book to the many nameless, faceless voices who deserve better.

Imagine being incarcerated for decades for a crime you did not commit. This book focuses, however, on those who find going through the civil legal system an insurmountable, daunting, and overwhelming task. Some of you are overwhelmed by the cost of litigation and hiring influential counsel to win your case and may be perplexed with why a system that should be accessible to all has so many hurdles to accessing justice. Finding funding to finance litigation is discussed.

This book further explains some court changes with self-help resources and law libraries. But that does not necessarily change who you may face in a courtroom and how that individual presides over a case. In this book, we share the differences between good and bad judges. For example, how is it that a judge who used a stun gun on a defendant was allowed to make it to the judiciary? We don't have the answers to this, but we understand how such a system that will enable this to happen remains in place.

Another question is why the judiciary isn't filled with the most brilliant legal minds to adjudicate cases fairly. For example, Equal Justice Initiative Executive Director Bryan Stevenson is an ideal choice for someone who should be serving on the U.S. Supreme Court. How can someone with such a brilliant legal mind and who has orchestrated cases causing the release of many wrongly convicted individuals not be considered for the highest judicial office in the land? It is time for the undervalued, marginalized population to be vocal about this.

The discussion also addresses the power of voters to elect fair judges. Just because sitting judges create signs telling you they are fair does not mean that is the case. We share briefly the election of judges and how that happens.

I am uniquely qualified to write this book because I have experienced injustice in the judicial system. I understand the politics of everything and the deficiencies in our legal and judicial system. I illuminate many injustices, including the rarity with which the U.S. Supreme Court hears many important cases brought before it. I hope you finish reading this book and never underestimate your voting power in electing the right judges to adjudicate cases fairly.

Chapter 1:

A Judge's Perspective on Why

People Sue or Are Sued

Understanding why people sue one another requires insight into the multifaceted nature of human interactions and the legal principles that govern them. From the vantage point of a judge, the courtroom is a microcosm of society's complexities, conflicts, and aspirations for justice. Lawsuits arise from broken promises, perceived injustices, unintentional harm, and deliberate wrongdoing. As a neutral arbiter, a judge encounters diverse cases, each shedding light on why individuals and entities find themselves entangled in legal disputes. This perspective provides a unique vantage point on the driving forces behind litigation, the societal norms at play, and the human behaviors that lead to legal actions. By examining these underlying factors, we gain a deeper appreciation for the judiciary's role in resolving conflicts and upholding the rule of law.

Anyone Can Be a Litigant

In the modern world, the principle of equality before the law is a cornerstone of democratic societies. The idea that anyone can be a litigant, regardless of race, creed, color, or religion, underscores the fundamental right of access to justice. This principle is enshrined in various national and international legal frameworks, promoting a fair and impartial legal system accessible to all.

Federal Judges Have Filed Lawsuits

In October 2012, the U.S. Court of Appeals for the Federal Circuit ordered Congress to pay federal judges six years of back pay (Holland, 2012). Another group of federal judges brought a class-action lawsuit to ensure that all of the federal judges who also missed out on their cost-of-living increases get their just compensation after the success of the previous lawsuit.

It's a touchy subject: One set of federal judges essentially asks another set to approve salary increases for everyone. Though, of course, Congress also ultimately controls its salaries. Congress in 1989 limited federal judges' ability to earn money outside of their work on the bench and, in exchange, provided what was supposed to be automatic cost-of-living increases to judicial salaries to ensure inflation wouldn't erode the value of those salaries over time (Holland, 2013).

Bad Things Happen to Good People

Some disputes cannot be settled short of filing a lawsuit. Many times, it is because the parties are unmovable in their positions. Whether it is a breach of contract case in which one party promised the other party something and never delivered it or an auto accident in which the parties cannot agree on who is at fault. The amount of compensation for personal injuries and lawsuits is a part of daily life.

Family Law

In family law matters, it may be the power dynamics of the relationship. Some men believe they are the head of the household, even if unmarried, and that role carries authoritative rights over women. The parties may clash if women don't follow that rule of authority. It may involve physical or verbal abuse or both. Such abuse may lead to the need for a peace order or protective order (Vogeler,

2019). Such protective orders in many jurisdictions are temporary. But you must know the law to prevail in these types of proceedings.

Many family law matters, such as lawsuits for custody, involve deception. The parties may not see it, but the judges presiding over these cases do see tit-for-tat behavior (Schepard, 2000). For example, suppose the parties do not have a custody order, and the separation just occurred. In that case, one parent may seize the opportunity to take the child away from a daycare before the other parent knows about it, which usually prompts emergency custody filings. Accusations of kidnapping and child abuse may then surface. The party who loses this custody battle feels disrespected and seeks revenge. This disrespect and revenge may play out in different ways. Some resort to violence. Others resort to tactics such as protracted litigation to outspend the other side.

Some parents refuse to pay child support. They would instead negotiate a deal to have joint and shared custody, where the child or children are with both parents for an even amount of time each week (O'Brien, 2021). The problem with this idea is that parents' work schedules may clash, or one parent may move away for a better position. Then the custody battle continues or falls apart. More changes in custody filings are likely. Some visitation battles are about keeping children after the visitation period ends in a custody order. Such battles again raise disrespect or even bullying and defiance of court orders.

Employment Disputes and Corporate Governance

Employment disputes come in many varieties. Some bosses can be overbearing or micromanaging to the dislike of subordinates.

Strong biases among many hiring officials affect how or whether they hire, promote, demote, or evaluate employees favorably or unfavorably. Incidents such as negative evaluations, firings, demotions, or employee misconduct such as sexual harassment may result in lawsuits based on wrongful discharge, sex or gender discrimination, constructive discharge, or breach of the employment contract (Pandya, 2012).

Litigation may ensue if a settlement agreement is reached and later breached. This type of breach could involve a party paying liquidated damages for breaching a confidentiality provision of a contract or involve a party indemnifying another party for breaching a nondisclosure agreement.

Millions of employers do not follow labor laws. They disobey laws by paying employees less than minimum wage, failing to pay employees overtime, using employment tests to exclude minority candidates who are otherwise qualified, terminating women who are pregnant because they are pregnant, etc. (Raghunandan, 2021).

In corporate governance matters, parties file lawsuits without succession plans, and leaders may disagree on who should succeed (Lederman, 2007). Churches file such disputes when a pastor dies, and there is no plan for future leadership.

Other examples of corporate battles include minority shareholder derivative suits. These are legal actions brought by shareholders on behalf of a corporation against its directors or officers, typically for misconduct such as breach of fiduciary duty, mismanagement, fraud, or self-dealing. These suits address wrongdoings that harm the corporation, with any monetary damages awarded going to the company rather than the individual shareholders (Garth et al., 1985). Shareholders often demand that the board rectify the issue, but they can bypass this step if they deem it futile. Successful suits can lead to financial compensation for the corporation and significant changes in corporate governance practices, serving as a crucial mechanism for maintaining accountability and integrity within corporate management.

Property Law, Deeds, and Real Estate

Adverse possession lawsuits also occur when property lines are in dispute and another party has recognized specific parcels of property for more than 20 years. Declaratory judgment actions or adverse possession actions may be required.

Many times, legal descriptions in deeds are not accurate. Metes and bounds surveys are required to learn of the discrepancy. Quiet title actions are widespread in resolving these disputes.

In real estate and construction law, parties may disagree on the contract terms when buying or constructing a house. If a performance bond is not in place and the general contractor stops working, more litigation may ensue. Mechanics liens are also part of civil litigation if a subcontractor, for example, was not paid for services rendered on property.

Guardianship Cases

Guardianship cases are a critical component of civil litigation, especially when individuals face incapacitation and cannot manage their affairs independently due to disability or other circumstances. In such instances, the legal system intervenes to protect the individual's interests by appointing a guardian. This guardian, appointed by the court, assumes responsibility for managing the person's well-being, property, or both aspects, depending on the specific needs and circumstances. This process ensures that vulnerable individuals receive the necessary care, support, and protection, safeguarding their rights and interests. Guardianship proceedings aim to balance the individual's autonomy with the need for intervention to ensure their safety and welfare (Näkki et al., 2024). Additionally, appointing a guardian involves careful consideration of the individual's best interests and may incorporate input from various stakeholders, including family members, medical professionals, and legal representatives. Guardianship cases play a vital role in upholding the rights and dignity of those incapacitated, providing essential support and oversight to ensure their well-being and security in navigating life's complexities.

Last Will and Testament and Estate Cases

When someone dies, the decedent's assets may require resolution and distribution by opening an estate. An estate opening may involve family disputes over who gets what. Sometimes, these battles are protracted, especially if immediate family members are not around to see and take care of the decedent during their last hours or period. States usually have laws of intestacy for those who die without a will; some do have a Last Will and Testament. Disagreements among family members may arise if immediate family or children are omitted from the will, potentially leading to a will contest challenging the mental capacity of the testator or person who drafted the will (Sneddon, 2011). It further raises questions of whether there was undue influence.

An Orphans Court or Register of Wills may handle estate matters. However, in some instances, cases resolved by an Orphans Court are appealed to the first trial court of jurisdiction.

Freedom of Information Act Cases

Some cases arise from the government's denial of access to public information. The Freedom of Information Act governs these cases, similar to laws in states, such as the Maryland Public Information Act (DPSCS, n.d.).

Consult a Lawyer Before Starting Litigation

I highly recommend consulting a lawyer before you file a lawsuit or take any initial steps as a pro se litigant if someone sues you. Many court systems have self-help resources, comprehensive law libraries, and lawyers who volunteer to assist litigants with how to file cases and handle defenses in cases.

You must ensure you finance any lawsuits adequately. If you decide to retain counsel, you can count on your opponent, if financially well off and motivated by revenge or disrespect, to outspend you in litigation costs.

Whether you are the plaintiff or defendant, the petitioner or respondent, most lawsuits are a matter of public record. Anyone, including news sources, can access your entire lawsuit unless subject to a protective order.

Beginning Your Lawsuit With a Complaint

If you cannot find a lawyer offering a free consultation, you may need to develop courage and a strategy to file your lawsuit. Start by visiting the state law library or self-help resources at local courts. Maryland's Law Library has a reliable resource called *Pleading Causes of Action* by Paul Mark Sandler, which allows you to understand what is needed to write your complaint. You must plead causes of action to form your complaint. Build your case, proving facts based on elements of a cause of action. For example, to plead a negligence case, you must prove there was a duty, a breach of that duty, causation, and damages.

Chapter 2:

The Judicial System Is Not Perfect

or Fair

Despite their shared commitment to impartially applying the law, judges do not uniformly think the same due to their diverse backgrounds, experiences, and judicial philosophies. Legal interpretation, personal background, judicial philosophy, precedent, policy considerations, and judicial discretion contribute to differences in judicial perspectives. While some judges may adhere strictly to precedent and legal principles, others may prioritize broader policy considerations or depart from precedent based on their interpretation of the law. These variations in judicial thinking underscore the legal system's complexity and highlight the importance of recognizing and understanding the diverse perspectives within the judiciary to ensure fair and just outcomes in court.

Judges, Tradition, and Social Media

The assumption that media sources like Fox News, MSNBC, CNN, Newsmax, talk shows, podcasts, and others have no influence on judges or that judges do not read newspapers is misguided. Like everyone else, judges are not immune to media and information's influence. Beyond traditional news outlets, judges also have access to the vast expanse of the internet, where information from various sources can shape their perspectives and understanding of current events and societal issues (Groves, 2021). Moreover, in today's digital age, judges may encounter information about litigants, cases, or legal matters through social media platforms or data leaks from third-party brokers. Even unintentional exposure to such information can subconsciously impact a judge's perceptions, potentially influencing their decisions in court. Therefore, it is essential for litigants and legal professionals to recognize the broader context within which judges operate and to exercise caution in their online activities to avoid any unintended consequences on the outcome of legal proceedings.

In the digital age, many judges maintain active social media accounts across various platforms, including Facebook, X (formerly known as Twitter), Instagram, and LinkedIn. While their usage may be limited or regulated, judges are vigilant in monitoring content on social media platforms. These accounts serve as windows into judges' personal and professional lives, offering glimpses into their interests, affiliations, and potential biases (Kurita, 2017). Although judges may exercise caution in their online interactions, they remain attentive to the information and discourse circulating within social media. Judges also tune into the broader online landscape, where discussions, opinions, and controversies can impact legal proceedings and public perceptions of the judiciary. As guardians of justice and arbiters of law, judges recognize the importance of maintaining impartiality and integrity in their online presence, navigating the digital realm with a keen understanding of its implications for the judicial process and the principles of fairness and equity. Thus, while social media may offer connectivity and engagement, judges navigate its terrain with a mindful balance of discretion, responsibility, and adherence to ethical standards, ensuring that their digital footprint upholds the dignity and impartiality of the judiciary.

Judges and Lawyers

Judges engage in conversations with their colleagues, providing an opportunity for information sharing about litigants, cases, and legal matters. During these discussions, judges may inadvertently learn details about individuals involved in litigation, including past litigants. This exchange of information presents a potential risk, as judges may form opinions about litigants based on secondhand knowledge without allowing them to address any misconceptions or inaccuracies (Geyh, 2014). For instance, a judge might refrain from explicitly stating that they have read news articles about a litigant and are using that information to shape their perception. However, if judges can access online content, including news articles or social media posts, they could absorb and internalize this information, influencing their views of the individuals involved in legal proceedings. This situation is concerning because it raises the possibility of unfair treatment or bias against litigants from incomplete or skewed information. It underscores the importance of maintaining transparency and impartiality in the judiciary and the need for litigants and legal professionals to be mindful of the potential impact of online content on judicial decision-making. In an era where digital information is readily accessible, safeguarding the integrity of the judicial process requires vigilance and awareness of the broader implications of judges' interactions and sources of information.

In addition to potential breaches of ethical conduct, judges may refrain from disclosing instances where they have engaged in ex parte communications with lawyers, including those representing either side of a case (Langs, 1997). Such interactions, where discussions occur outside the presence of all parties involved, raise concerns regarding impartiality and fairness in legal proceedings. If judges know that admitting to these communications would violate ethics rules, they may opt not to disclose them. So, you cannot count on the Commission on Judicial Disabilities to hold all judges accountable. My experience is that they rarely do. Examine the composition of these Commissions on Judicial Disabilities to determine whether they are political appointments or open to public applications and consideration.

Moreover, such actions undermine the principles of transparency and accountability that are fundamental to the administration of justice. Therefore, judges must ensure that their actions align with the principles of fairness, impartiality, and integrity, upholding the highest standards of ethical conduct. Any deviation from these principles jeopardizes the legitimacy of judicial decisions and undermines society's foundational values of justice and equity.

Judges and Their Biases and Convictions

Don't assume judges are not biased or have strong convictions. Don't even assume all judges are ethical. Some engage in underhanded tactics, such as scheduling orders that favor one litigant over the other. Even today, some legal analysts criticize Judge Aileen Cannon for her handling of the classified documents case in the *United States v. Donald J. Trump et al.* in Florida. They have accused her of delaying the proceedings, resulting in the absence of a trial date before the November 2024 general elections (Mangan, 2024). Accusers allege that even the United States Supreme Court intentionally scheduled the case addressing the issue of presidential immunity until mid-summer 2024 to avoid interfering with many primary presidential elections in 2024.

Many judges have implicit biases, which manifest in being culturally conditioned not to accept credible black litigants versus white litigants. The same is true about not accepting citizen statements over police statements. Some give greater weight to police statements. Others administer justice unevenly when police receive criminal charges. The biggest concern is not removing such judges with these established biases.

I recall when I ran in a contested judicial election in 2016, one sitting judge misrepresented to voters during the primary election that I was not a judge, even though I was (Weathers, 2016). Nothing happened to him. So, you cannot count on the Commission on Judicial Disabilities to hold judges accountable. They won't.

Don't Assume Our Judicial System Is Fair

Also, don't assume our judicial system is fair and renders justice. Consider the case of Sergeant Isaac Woodard. He was a black World War II veteran who returned to the United States after serving in World War II for 3 ½ years. The Batesburg, South Carolina, police chief allegedly beat him. The police chief allegedly plunged a blackjack in each of Woodard's eye sockets, blinding him (Waxman, 2021).

Those who held Woodard in custody arrested him. Later, they threw whiskey on him to make it appear as though Sergeant Woodard was drunk or had been drinking. Eventually, authorities charged Batesburg Police Chief Lynwood Schull with violating Sergeant Woodard's civil rights by blinding his eyes. Judge J. Waties Waring, the son of a Confederate soldier, presided over the case in November 1946 (Waxman, 2021). An all-white jury deliberated for 15 minutes, acquitting Schull. This is another example of an Emmett Till verdict.

Jury Pools

Don't assume jury pools are fair and impartial. None of my immediate family members, who have resided in Maryland for at least six decades, have been called for a federal jury in Maryland. All of us are registered voters with no criminal records. There are still instances in Maryland of all white juries rendering verdicts acquitting police of misconduct. Consider the case of *Towhee Sparrow v. City of Annapolis* in the U.S. District Court for the District of Maryland (Cook, 2016). An all-white jury acquitted police of misconduct on June 6, 2018.

Chapter 3:

The Pro Se Litigant Versus the Represented Litigant – A Judge's Perception

Representing oneself in court, known as pro se representation, carries a unique set of advantages and disadvantages from a judge's perspective. On the one hand, judges recognize the potential benefits, such as cost savings for defendants who might not be able to afford legal counsel and the opportunity for individuals to articulate their cases directly. However, judges also face challenges with pro se litigants, including potential delays in proceedings due to the individual's lack of legal expertise, which can lead to procedural errors and misunderstandings of court rules (Cooper, 2023). Balancing the right to self-representation with the need for efficient and fair administration of justice presents a nuanced and complex dynamic in the courtroom.

Pro Se Litigant Credibility

When a judge evaluates the legal arguments presented by a pro se litigant, the standard is generally consistent with that applied to arguments made by attorneys. However, judges may extend a degree of leniency to pro se litigants, recognizing their lack of formal legal training. This leniency can manifest in allowing more explanation time, forgiving procedural errors, and sometimes guiding legal procedures and requirements. Nevertheless, the substantive legal arguments must still meet the required legal standards. Judges strive to maintain fairness and impartiality, upholding the pro se litigant's rights while preserving the legal process's integrity and efficiency.

Resources for Pro Se Litigants

Pro se litigants can access various resources to help them navigate the legal system. These resources include (ABA, n.d.-b):

- **Court Websites and Online Resources:**

  - **State and Federal Court Websites:** Many court websites offer self-help sections with guides, forms, and instructional videos. For example, the United States Courts website provides resources for federal cases.

  - **Legal Aid Websites:** Websites like Legal Aid Society and LawHelp.org offer information on common legal issues, form templates, and directories of legal aid providers.

  - **Public Legal Education Websites:** Nolo and FindLaw provide articles, legal dictionaries, and Q&A sections on various legal topics.

  - **Online Legal Libraries:** Platforms like Google Scholar offer access to a vast case law database, legal articles, and other legal documents.

- **Court Libraries:**

  - **Public Law Libraries:** Most courts have law libraries open to the public, offering access to legal texts, case reporters, statutes, and other reference materials. Librarians are often available to assist with locating resources.

- o **Self-Help Centers:** Many courts have established self-help centers or clinics within the courthouse, staffed with volunteers or legal professionals who can guide legal procedures, form completion, and essential legal advice.

- **Local Bar Associations:**

  - o **Pro Bono Services:** Many local bar associations offer pro bono (free) legal services or clinics where volunteer attorneys provide brief consultations or assist with document preparation.

  - o **Lawyer Referral** Services: Bar associations often provide referral services to help pro se litigants find affordable legal representation or advice.

- **Community Organizations and Nonprofits:**

  - o **Legal Aid Organizations:** Organizations such as Legal Services Corporation and local legal aid societies offer eligible individuals free or low-cost legal assistance.

  - o **Nonprofit Organizations:** Various nonprofits focus on specific areas of law, such as tenant rights, family law, or immigration, providing targeted resources and support.

By utilizing these resources, pro se litigants can better understand the legal process, prepare their cases, and effectively represent themselves in court.

Pro Se Litigants and the Rule of the Court

Judges expect pro se litigants to familiarize themselves with the court's rules. While judges may offer some leniency to individuals representing themselves, it is ultimately the responsibility of the litigant to understand and adhere to court procedures and legal requirements. This expectation includes knowing how to file documents properly, meet deadlines, present evidence, and follow courtroom protocol (Hammond, 2022).

Judges emphasize the importance of this familiarity for several reasons:

- **Efficiency and Fairness:** Understanding court rules helps ensure that proceedings run smoothly and efficiently, minimizing delays and disruptions. It also ensures fairness to all parties involved, including those represented by attorneys.

- **Legal Standards:** Regardless of representation, all parties must meet specific legal standards. Familiarity with court rules helps pro se litigants present their cases effectively and meet these standards.

- **Judicial Neutrality:** While judges aim to be fair and may provide some guidance to pro se litigants, they must remain neutral and cannot act as legal advisors. Therefore, litigants must take the initiative to understand the rules.

To assist pro se litigants, courts often provide resources such as:

- **Self-Help Guides and FAQs:** Many court websites offer detailed guides and FAQs on court procedures.

- **Workshops and Clinics:** Some courts offer workshops or clinics to help pro se litigants understand specific aspects of the legal process.

- **Court Staff Assistance:** Court clerks and self-help center staff can provide information and answer questions about court procedures (though they cannot offer legal advice).

Despite these resources, the onus remains on the pro se litigant to make an effort to understand and comply with the court's rules.

Chapter 4:

The Justice System Has Good and

Bad Judges

The justice system, a cornerstone of societal order and fairness, is often scrutinized for its ability to deliver impartial justice. Yet the reality reveals a complex landscape where the quality of justice can vary significantly, hinging largely on the judges who preside over cases. On the one hand, good judges, characterized by their fairness, integrity, and adherence to the law, strive to uphold the principles of justice and equality. Conversely, bad judges, who may be biased, incompetent, or corrupt, can undermine the very foundation of the judicial system. This dichotomy highlights the justice system's inherent imperfections, illustrating how exemplary and flawed judges can result in experiences of profound fairness or stark injustice for those seeking legal redress.

Good Judges and Their Qualities

Good judges play a crucial role in upholding the justice system's integrity through their actions and demeanor. Among their key qualities are being active listeners and showing respect for litigants. These attributes foster a fair courtroom environment and effectively serve justice.

Active Listening

A good judge exemplifies active listening, which involves fully concentrating, understanding, and responding thoughtfully to both parties. This skill ensures thorough consideration of all arguments and evidence. By paying close attention to the details presented by both parties, active listeners can make well-informed decisions based on the case's merits rather than superficial impressions (Reyes, 2021). Active listening also helps judges catch nuances and subtleties that may be pivotal in understanding the context and relevance of the presented information, leading to more accurate and just rulings.

Respect for Litigants

Respecting litigants, regardless of their background or status, is another hallmark of a good judge. This respect manifests in several ways (Lagratta, 2015):

- **Fair Treatment:** Good judges ensure that all litigants receive equal treatment and consideration, help to build trust in the judicial process, and reinforce the principle of equality before the law.

- **Clear Communication:** Judges who respect litigants take the time to explain legal procedures, rulings, and the reasoning behind their decisions in clear, understandable terms. This transparency helps litigants feel heard and valued, even if the outcome is not in their favor.

- **Patience and Empathy:** Recognizing that court proceedings can be stressful and intimidating, good judges exhibit patience and empathy. They allow litigants to present their cases fully without unnecessary interruption or dismissiveness.

These qualities of good judges contribute to a judicial process that all participants perceive as fair and just. Judges help uphold the court's dignity and the legal system by actively listening and respecting litigants.

Bad Judges and Their Qualities

The Word Press presents a blog of the Center for Judicial Ethics of the National Center for State Courts each week. This blog details the number of disciplinary actions taken against judges. They vary from judges reprimanded for abuses of power and lying to investigators to judges charged with DUIs.

While good judges uphold the principles of fairness and respect within the judicial system, bad judges can significantly undermine these principles through negative behaviors and attitudes. Judges with short, curt, and rude temperaments who frequently interrupt litigants before fully presenting their points create a very intimidating courtroom environment. Is this intimidation necessary or unnecessary?

Short, Curt, and Rude Temperament

Judges with short and curt demeanor often appear impatient and dismissive. This attitude can be particularly damaging in a courtroom where litigants may already feel vulnerable and anxious. A rude temperament further exacerbates this issue, leading to a lack of respect and trust in the judicial process (Maroney, 2021). Such behavior can make litigants feel belittled and unheard, undermining their confidence in receiving a fair hearing.

Interrupting Litigants

Frequent interruptions by a judge prevent litigants from fully articulating their arguments and presenting their evidence, which not only hampers the litigants' ability to make their case but also leads to the consideration of incomplete information in the decision-making process. When judges interrupt, they may miss critical details and nuances essential for a fair and accurate ruling.

The judge's attitude impacts the courtroom atmosphere in the following ways:

- **Perception of Bias:** Judges who are rude and interruptive may be perceived as biased, favoring one party. This perception can erode trust in the impartiality of the court.

- **Reduced Confidence in the Legal System:** Litigants who experience such behavior may lose faith in the justice system, feeling that it is more about the judge's disposition than the law's fair and objective application.

- **Stress and Intimidation:** A hostile courtroom environment can increase stress and intimidation for litigants, particularly those unfamiliar with legal procedures or representing themselves, and can lead to poor presentation of their case and, ultimately, unjust outcomes.

Additionally, this behavior can discourage litigants from fully engaging in the process, feeling that their voices are not valued or respected.

Appeals and Mistrust

Decisions made by judges with poor temperaments are more likely to be appealed, leading to increased caseloads and delays in the judicial system. This mistrust can have broader implications, diminishing public confidence in the legal system's ability to deliver justice.

Overall, bad judges who exhibit these negative traits compromise the fairness and integrity of the judicial process. They create an environment where litigants feel disrespected and unheard, ultimately undermining the very foundation of justice. The judicial system must address such behaviors to ensure everyone receives a fair and respectful hearing.

Judges Under Fire

In recent times, the actions and decisions of judges have come under intense scrutiny and criticism, raising significant concerns about the integrity and impartiality of the judiciary. This surge in public and political scrutiny stems from controversial rulings and perceived biases that have fueled judicial conduct and accountability debates. Judges, as the cornerstone of the legal system, must uphold the highest standards of fairness and justice; however, when people question their actions, it shakes the foundation of public trust in the judicial process. Here, we explore the multifaceted reasons behind the growing criticism of judges, the implications for the legal system, and potential measures to restore confidence in judicial fairness and objectivity.

Judge Robert K. Adrian

In May 2024, Adams County Judge Robert Adrian faced disciplinary action following a controversial decision in a sexual assault case that had previously attracted significant public attention. The complaint against Judge Adrian stemmed from his January 2022 decision to overturn the conviction of an 18-year-old accused of raping a 16-year-old girl, despite initially finding the defendant guilty. Adrian justified the reversal because he claimed the 148 days the defendant had already spent in jail was a sufficient sentence, a decision that sparked widespread criticism (Smith, 2024).

During a three-day hearing in November 2023, the Judicial Inquiry Board reviewed the complaint against Judge Adrian. On the following Friday, May 2024, the Board decided after careful deliberation. Judge Adrian was reprimanded for his conduct, specifically citing concerns about his impartiality and adherence to judicial ethics (Bethune, 2024). The Board's decision highlighted the importance of maintaining public trust in the judiciary and ensuring that judges uphold the principles of fairness and justice without yielding to personal biases or external pressures.

This case underscores the critical role of judicial oversight bodies in maintaining the integrity of the legal system and holding judges accountable for their decisions. The Board's actions reflect a commitment to upholding ethical standards within the judiciary, ensuring all individuals receive fair treatment under the law.

Judge Aaron Persky

The Brock Turner case, a 2015 sexual assault involving a Stanford University student and an unconscious woman, gained national attention due to its lenient sentencing and subsequent recall of Judge Aaron Persky. Turner was convicted of three felony sexual assault counts yet received only a six-month jail sentence, sparking outrage over what many perceived as a failure of justice. Judge Persky's decision to impose a light sentence, citing Turner's lack of criminal history and potential impact on his future, led to widespread criticism and activism.

In response, a campaign led by Stanford law professor Michele Dauber called for Judge Persky's recall, arguing that his lenient sentencing reflected biases and failed to address sexual violence adequately (Helsel, 2019). This movement gained momentum, resulting in a special recall election in 2018, where voters overwhelmingly supported Judge Persky's removal from the bench. The case and subsequent recall highlighted issues of judicial accountability, sentencing reform in sexual assault cases, and the power of public advocacy in promoting justice for survivors.

Judge Robert C. Nalley

Judge Robert C. Nalley of the Charles County Circuit Court in Maryland is a figure who has garnered attention for his controversial actions and decisions. Over the years, several incidents involving him have sparked debate and criticism.

One notable incident occurred in 2014 when Judge Nalley ordered a deputy to shock a defendant with a stun cuff during a court proceeding. The defendant, Delvon L. King, was representing himself in a gun case and repeatedly refused to stop talking when instructed by the judge. Nalley ordered the deputy to activate the stun cuff, which delivered an electric shock to King (Castaneda, 2016). This action led to significant backlash, and in 2016, Nalley pleaded guilty to a misdemeanor civil rights violation for this incident. He was sentenced to a year of probation and ordered to take anger management classes.

In 2010, Judge Nalley received a suspension after authorities found him responsible for deflating the tires of a courthouse cleaning worker's car (LaFleur, 2010). He admitted to this act, stating that the worker had parked in a restricted area. This incident led to a temporary suspension from the bench and mandatory anger management counseling.

These incidents have significantly impacted Nalley's reputation, raising questions about his judicial temperament and respect for defendants' rights. His actions have been viewed as abuses of power, leading to disciplinary actions and legal consequences. Critics argue that such behavior undermines public confidence in the judicial system and highlights the importance of accountability and proper conduct among those who hold judicial office.

Judge Jonathan Newell

Judge Jonathan Newell served as Caroline County's state attorney in 2003 and became a Caroline County Circuit Court Judge in Maryland in 2016. In 2021, he committed suicide before the FBI could arrest him on federal charges of sexual exploitation of a child. He swallowed a piece of evidence, a camera memory card, before committing suicide; however, federal and state officials do not believe he distributed the images (Judge Jonathan Newell, 2021). With Newell's death, the state's attorney turned resources toward helping the victims.

It's important to note that Newell was never found guilty of sexual exploitation of a child; there was only a federal criminal complaint filed against him by FBI Special Agent Rachel S. Corn (Jones, 2021). With his death, the investigators found videos of Newell allegedly touching minors and videos of minors showering. Newell, escaping justice through death, left his victims with no closure—a stark example of justice not being served.

Chapter 5:

Judicial Reform in How Judges are

Chosen

The process of selecting judges and the ongoing efforts toward judicial reform are critical components in maintaining the integrity and effectiveness of the judicial system. Different jurisdictions choose judges using various methods, including elections, appointments, and merit-based selections. Each technique aims to balance judicial independence with accountability yet faces its own set of challenges and criticisms. Judicial reform initiatives address these issues by improving transparency, reducing political influence, and ensuring the judiciary remains fair and impartial. Understanding the mechanisms behind judge selection and the need for reform is essential for fostering a legal system that upholds justice and public confidence.

History of the Judiciary Selection System

The history of states selecting judges is a complex narrative shaped by various political, social, and legal factors. Traditionally, judicial selection methods have evolved alongside broader changes in governance structures and societal norms (Tuskai, 2021):

- **Colonial Era:** During the early colonial period of America, colonial governors or other executive authorities often appointed judges, reflecting colonial governance's hierarchical and centralized nature.

- **Jacksonian Era and the Rise of Popular Democracy:** The Jacksonian era in the 19th century witnessed a shift toward popular democracy and the expansion of voting. This period saw the emergence of judicial elections as a method of selecting judges in many states. The idea was to make judges more directly accountable to the people.

- **Progressive Era Reforms:** In the late 19th and early 20th centuries, the Progressive movement spurred reforms to curb corruption and improve governance. This era saw the adoption of merit-based selection systems in some states, such as the Missouri Plan, which aimed to balance judicial independence with accountability.

- **20th Century Trends:** Throughout the 20th century, states experimented with various judicial selection methods, including appointments, elections, and hybrid systems. The balance between political accountability and judicial independence remained a central theme in these discussions.

Contemporary Debates

Nowadays, debates over judicial selection continue, with proponents of different methods arguing for their advantages. Many praise appointment systems for ensuring qualified judges and insulating the judiciary from political pressures; however, they can also raise concerns about the lack of democratic accountability (Celeste, 2010). Conversely, elections are seen as a means of ensuring democratic legitimacy but can lead to politicization of the judiciary and potential conflicts of interest.

Calls for Reform

In recent years, a growing chorus of advocates has demanded substantial reforms to the judicial selection processes across various jurisdictions. These calls have intensified due to mounting concerns regarding the detrimental impacts of partisanship, the undue influence of special interests, and the crucial need to safeguard judicial independence. Recognizing the imperative to fortify the judiciary's integrity, some states have enacted significant reforms to revitalize the selection process. These reforms have been multifaceted, focusing on bolstering transparency to illuminate the often opaque selection procedures, curbing the pervasive influence of political agendas to uphold the judiciary's impartiality, and prioritizing diversity initiatives to ensure equitable representation on the bench (Czarnezki, 2005). By implementing these reforms, states endeavor to cultivate a judiciary that is more accountable, impartial, and reflective of the diverse communities it serves, thereby fostering greater public trust in the judicial system.

Methods of Judicial Selection

Unlike state courts, federal judicial selection carries a unique pathway to the federal bench. Some lawyers apply to serve as a federal magistrate judge. The district court panel of judges chooses these magistrate judges using a merit selection panel. A panel of U.S. Circuit-level judges usually selects bankruptcy court judges.

Other lawyers approach senior U.S. senators in their states to express their interest in serving on the federal bench. The White House receives a referral, interviews the candidate, and conducts background checks. The U.S. Senator plays a vital role in the blue slip process of approving the judge's choice. The president nominates, the Senate Judicial Committee conducts hearings on candidates, and only the U.S. Senate confirms judicial nominees.

Judicial selection methods vary significantly across different jurisdictions, each with its unique approach to appointing judges. The primary methods include elections, appointments, and merit-based selections, each with advantages and drawbacks.

Nonpartisan and Partisan Elections

Partisan elections represent a significant departure from the traditional image of judicial independence, as they introduce overt political affiliations into the selection process. In this system, judicial candidates align themselves explicitly with political parties, mirroring the campaign strategies of other elected officials. While this approach ostensibly promotes democratic participation by allowing voters to make informed choices based on party affiliation, it also introduces a host of concerns regarding the politicization of the judiciary. By intertwining judicial selection with partisan politics, judges may feel pressured to align their decisions with the ideological agendas of their affiliated party rather than adjudicating cases strictly on legal merits. This erosion of judicial impartiality undermines the fundamental principle of the rule of law and compromises public trust in the judiciary's ability to administer justice impartially (Kang & Shepherd, 2011). Moreover, partisan elections often incentivize candidates to prioritize fundraising and campaign strategies over legal expertise and judicial temperament, further diluting the quality and integrity of the judiciary. Consequently, while partisan elections may offer a semblance of democratic participation, they come at the cost of jeopardizing the foundational principles of an independent and impartial judiciary.

Nonpartisan elections represent an attempt to divorce judicial selection from overt partisan affiliations, thereby ostensibly preserving the impartiality and integrity of the judiciary. In these elections, candidates for judicial positions eschew party labels, emphasizing their qualifications, experience, and judicial philosophy. By removing overt partisan cues from the electoral process, nonpartisan elections prioritize merit-based considerations and promote public confidence in the judiciary's ability to dispense justice fairly and impartially (Ash & MacLeod, 2021). However, despite these noble intentions, nonpartisan elections are not immune to challenges and criticisms. While they may mitigate the overt politicization of the judiciary, concerns persist regarding the potential for hidden biases and influence to shape judicial campaigns. Despite operating without partisan banners, special interest groups may still wield considerable influence by mobilizing resources and shaping public opinion through campaign contributions and advocacy efforts. Additionally, the absence of party labels does not guarantee that voters will be fully informed about candidates' judicial philosophies or potential biases, potentially undermining the effectiveness of nonpartisan elections in safeguarding judicial impartiality. Thus, while nonpartisan elections represent a step toward depoliticizing judicial selection, they must be accompanied by robust transparency measures and public education initiatives to ensure that voters can make informed decisions and uphold the judiciary's independence and integrity.

Executive and Legislative Appointments

In the executive appointments method, the responsibility for appointing judges falls squarely on the shoulders of a governor or president, typically with the requirement of advice and consent from a legislative body, often the Senate. This approach is frequently lauded for its potential to facilitate thorough vetting processes, ensuring that appointed judges are highly qualified and possess the requisite expertise and integrity to serve on the bench effectively. By subjecting nominees to scrutiny by both the executive and legislative branches, executive appointments provide a robust system of checks and balances, helping to safeguard against the appointment of unsuitable candidates. However, despite these purported benefits, the executive appointments method has drawbacks. One significant concern is the potential for political favoritism to influence the selection process, with governors or presidents appointing judges based on partisan allegiance rather than merit. The involvement of elected officials exacerbates this risk, as they may prioritize political considerations over qualifications when evaluating judicial nominees.

Additionally, the lack of transparency in the executive appointments method can undermine public confidence in the judiciary's independence and impartiality. The closed-door nature of the selection process may foster perceptions of backroom deals and cronyism, further eroding trust in the judiciary's integrity (Ware, 2022). Consequently, while executive appointments offer the potential for thorough vetting and the appointment of highly qualified judges, policymakers must remain vigilant in addressing concerns about political influence and transparency to uphold the integrity and legitimacy of the judicial selection process.

In the legislative appointments method, the responsibility for selecting judges lies directly with a legislative body, a state legislature, or parliament. This approach serves as a crucial check on executive power, ensuring that the executive branch does not solely dictate the judiciary's composition. By vesting the authority to appoint judges in the legislature, proponents argue that this method helps to distribute power more evenly across branches of government, preventing any single branch from monopolizing control over judicial appointments. However, despite these purported advantages, the legislative appointments method has challenges. One significant concern is the potential for highly politicized selections, as legislators may be influenced by partisan agendas or special interest groups when appointing judges (Bannon, 2016). The politicization of the judicial selection process can undermine public confidence in the judiciary's impartiality and independence, as it may lead to the perception that judges are beholden to the interests of the legislative body that appointed them. Additionally, the concentration of appointment power within the legislature may raise questions about the judiciary's ability to check legislative authority, potentially compromising the separation of powers essential for maintaining democratic governance. Consequently, while legislative appointments offer a mechanism for balancing executive power, policymakers must carefully consider the risks of politicization and safeguard judicial independence to ensure the judiciary's integrity and uphold the rule of law.

Merit-Based Selection

The merit-based selection system, often called the Missouri Plan, represents a unique approach to judicial selection that seeks to balance judicial independence and public accountability. This method's core is a nonpartisan commission that rigorously evaluates judicial candidates based on their qualifications, experience, and temperament.

This commission reviews the candidates' backgrounds and legal understanding, ensuring that it considers only the most qualified individuals for judicial appointment. Once the commission completes its assessment, it provides the executive with a shortlist of recommended candidates, thereby insulating the selection process from overt political influence. However, unlike traditional appointment systems, the merit-based selection system incorporates a mechanism for public oversight by subjecting appointed judges to retention elections after a designated service period (Caufield, 2010). During these retention elections, voters can evaluate the performance of sitting judges and decide whether they should remain in office. This dual-layered approach to judicial selection promotes transparency and accountability and guards against the undue influence of partisan politics. By empowering independent commissions to evaluate judicial candidates based on merit and subjecting appointed judges to periodic public scrutiny, the merit-based selection system ensures that the judiciary remains impartial, competent, and responsive to the community's needs.

Hybrid Systems

In response to different jurisdictions' diverse needs and contexts, some regions have adopted hybrid methods combining appointments, elections, and merit-based selection elements. These hybrid systems leverage each approach's advantages while mitigating their drawbacks. In one standard hybrid model, an executive or legislative process appoints judges, enabling thorough vetting and ensuring the selection of qualified candidates for the bench. However, unlike traditional appointment systems, judges appointed under this hybrid model are subsequently subjected to retention elections after serving a designated period. During these retention elections, voters can assess the judges' performance and decide whether they should remain in office. This hybrid approach effectively combines the benefits of appointment-based selection, which prioritizes qualifications and expertise, with the accountability mechanisms inherent in electoral systems (Anastopoulo & Cooks III, 2013). By blending these elements, hybrid systems balance judicial independence and public oversight, promoting transparency, accountability, and public confidence in the judiciary. Additionally, the flexibility of hybrid methods allows jurisdictions to tailor their judicial selection processes to their unique circumstances and preferences, ensuring that they can adapt to evolving needs and challenges while upholding the judiciary's integrity.

Considerations and Reforms

Each method of judicial selection comes with inherent strengths and weaknesses. Ongoing judicial reform efforts focus on enhancing transparency, reducing political and special interest influence, and ensuring that the judiciary remains impartial and competent. These reforms often advocate for methods that balance judicial independence and accountability to maintain public trust in the judicial system.

Contested Judicial Elections

In Maryland, only judges in Maryland's circuit courts may find themselves running in contested judicial elections. After going through the trial court judicial nominating process and being interviewed by the governor, the governor appoints circuit court judges; however, they must run to be elected by the people, which is good. Many judges appointed do not display their biases in a judicial nominating commission or voluntary bar association interview. Most judicial candidates interviewed tell the panel what they want to hear. Be careful how you choose judges when at the ballot box. Many appointed candidates can be beholden to the governor and those in his or her political circles. Those who are not appointed may not be.

Citizens should understand that eliminating contested judicial elections will suppress voter rights by removing the right of citizens to vote for their judges. The status quo system wants to replace the voter's choice way with a retention election where voters can only approve who the establishment has chosen as your circuit court judges. This change is significant because the judicial terms are 15 years in Maryland. If the law were changed to retention elections, voters could only rubber stamp those judges nominated by the judicial nominating commission. This possible change is a concern because many judges prefer not to run because they don't want to meet the public and community leaders. They prefer to live in a bubble and not meet the public. Too many judges are arrogant and out of touch with human beings. They would rather define litigants based on their misguided cultural preconceived notions of litigants.

A Look Into the Maryland Circuit Courts

The problem is that racial politics are still in play in many counties across the state of Maryland, and the nominating commissions have poor track records. These racial politics play on prejudices and stereotypes. Once nominated, the incumbent judges have an advantage and give the appearance that the nominating commissions vetted them; therefore, they are the better candidates. Still, no one is looking closely at the track record of the commissions, nor are the commissions being held to an equity standard.

In 2016, Reverend Rickey Nelson Jones and I ran in a contested judicial election for Anne Arundel County Circuit Court judge in Maryland. There were many underhanded tactics used.

When I filed my certificate of candidacy, the Anne Arundel County Circuit Court had consisted of an all-white judiciary for over a decade (2005-2016). For over 11 years, no woman of color ever received an appointment to this bench. The Judicial Nominating Commission had no shame about keeping things this way when they only shortlisted white applicants for more than a decade for judicial vacancies on this court (Barber, 2021). Governors were complicit in this shortlisting of whites by stacking the judicial nominating commissions with majority white members. At that time, I was a sitting administrative law judge with 10 years of judicial experience and over 5,000 judicial opinions to my credit.

Reverend Jones filed a lawsuit against Maryland's Administrative Office of Courts challenging the racial inequities in Anne Arundel County's judiciary system, except this fight for justice was dismissed.

Once the right to elect trial court judges in an open process is closed, voters will likely never get the right to vote in a contested judicial election ever again. This closure places too much control in the hands of primarily white governors and legislators. Voters, in reality, are robbed of their opportunity to weigh in on who serves as their trial court judges. They lose the right to decide who presides over critical matters like sentencing and weighing the credibility of witnesses such as police officers and other law enforcement that significantly impact the community.

Voters would then face only the option of voting yes or no to retain a judge, with no opportunity to select an alternative candidate. The power to choose a judge is enormous. These judges decide if law enforcement should be held accountable for police misconduct. Circuit court judges are in office for 15 years and will impact thousands of laws and lives, and they can and will set precedents that will stay in place for decades.

Judicial Reform

Many write about the current topic of police reform since George Floyd's death, but judicial reform is also fundamental. Why are white judges telling the minority population what discrimination looks like and what is needed to prove a discrimination case? The wrong people are controlling the narrative. White bureaucrats, white hearing officers, and white judges have lowered the standard of proof and made it easier to find sex discrimination and almost impossible to find a case of race discrimination.

That is why having a diverse judiciary and government matters; it impacts perspective. The Maryland State Commission on Criminal Sentencing Policy disclosed the following (2023):

In calendar years 2018 through 2020, the majority (63.4%) of guidelines-sentenced individuals were Black. In comparison, 29% of sentenced individuals were White, 6.2% were Hispanic, and 1.4% were of an Other race. Relative to the other judicial circuits, the 8th Circuit accounted for the largest percentage of Black guidelines-sentenced individuals (90.3%), while the 6th Circuit accounted for the largest percentage of Hispanic individuals (18.2%). Guidelines-eligible sentencing events in the 2nd Circuit were comprised of the largest percentage of White individuals (60.9%) relative to other judicial circuits, though the total number of sentencing events in the 2nd Circuit was comparatively small. (p. 2)

When a judicial system waits 368 years to place a woman of color, a Hispanic, a Native American, or an Asian American on its trial court bench, that system has already shown you who they are. The bold practice of exclusion with no consequences is self-evident. The system has no shame—nor is it subject to any accountability, and it revels in its pride of abuse.

The Anne Arundel County, Maryland Judicial System

The judicial system in Anne Arundel County, Maryland, should be ashamed because there are no black men on this Circuit Court.

The last African-American male judge, Rodney Warren, was voted out of office in 2005. Statistics are even worse for Hispanics, Native Americans, Asian Americans, and Pacific Islanders. There are no non-white male judges on this Circuit Court bench in 2024. The same is true of other counties in Maryland, with some having no minority representation. People of color head less than 50% of the 24 Circuit Courts, leading only eight of the Circuit Courts in Maryland (Distribution of Judges, 2023). The disparities among judicial opinions arise because judges do not consider systemic issues due to the lack of representation.

Judicial reform is long overdue. A key concern is that more transparency is needed to remove conflicts of interest and the appearance of impropriety that may arise when deciding on nomination recommendations. Another area of concern is establishing objective and consistent evaluation criteria. For example, every judicial nominee should be evaluated on their knowledge of sentencing disparities and explain how their record demonstrates that they do not have a track record of encouraging such inequality and how they will work to address such disparities if selected for the judicial position proactively (Barber, 2021).

In 2018, Governor Larry Hogan appointed the first African-American female to the Anne Arundel County Circuit Court (Felice, 2018). This appointment was a historic moment that came after many civil rights organizations such as the Anne Arundel County NAACP, Showing Up for Racial Justice, and the Caucus of African-American Leaders staged formal protests in front of the circuit court for Anne Arundel County at 8 Church Circle, Annapolis, Maryland. In my opinion, after Judge Elizabeth Morris' appointment, Governor Hogan's trial court judicial nominating committee, as well as the appellate judicial nominating committee, went right back to practicing exclusionary tactics when shortlisting applicants for the trial court and appellate benches in Anne Arundel County (Barber, 2021). The fact that no people of color, specifically zero, made the shortlist from 2018 through 2022 supports this conclusion. It should be noted that many of the applicants of color had significantly more experience than the white nominees selected for referral to the governor.

In 2024, Governor Wes Moore appointed Ginina Jackson-Stevenson as only the second African-American female judge on the circuit court for Anne Arundel County (Munro, 2023).

Despite the apparent lack of diversity in the Maryland judiciary, the former chief judge of the Court of Appeals of Maryland, Mary Ellen Barbera, has endorsed eliminating contested judicial elections. Year after year, Chief Judge Barbera brought in a few African-American judges from various jurisdictions around the state to testify before the state legislature—who happened to get nominated in jurisdictions to encourage legislators to co-sponsor legislation eliminating contested judicial elections.

Racial Discrimination and Judicial Reform

When evaluating race discrimination fairly, the adjudicator or a skilled jurist considers that racism is often invisible and manifests with hidden agendas. The hidden agenda could be white supremacy, which is shown in the sentencing disparity reports as outlined above. Only these skilled jurists are qualified to serve in courts, and they are rarely there.

For example, in 1980, former judge and now managing law partner William Murphy, Jr., who represented the family of Freddie Gray, ran in a contested judicial election on the circuit court for Baltimore City (Billy Murphy, n.d.). He has one of the most brilliant legal minds in this country. He would not have served on this trial court if it were not for the contested judicial election process. The case of William Murphy, Jr. shows why the judicial nomination process does not work. It bypasses brilliant lawyers every day. What voter would want a presidential nominating commission to decide who you should pick as president of the United States?

Judicial nominating commissions are also a failed process because politics drive these commissions, and they practice exclusion, like the trial court judicial nomination commission in Anne Arundel County did from 2005 through 2017, as noted above. The statistical data mentioned above also demonstrates that many counties in Maryland miss opportunities to appoint Native Americans, Hispanic Americans, and others to the bench. Even in the heavily populated Montgomery County, the circuit court has no African-American males on the bench in 2024. This lack of representation is not by accident. Social justice advocates are also mindful that having minority representation is not always the solution when the minority chosen supports the status quo. This, too, is problematic.

Understanding Discrimination

Just about every facet of life is racialized because racism is the source of problems involved in almost everything we do in life. It impacts how we pick judges. It also involves who gets street lights in specific communities or who gets better educational funding. Historically black colleges and universities (HBCUs) in Maryland recently settled a long-standing case regarding underfunding compared to white institutions of higher learning.

Lawyers' Committee for Civil Rights

The Lawyers' Committee for Civil Rights has steadfastly advocated for equity and justice in education, mainly focusing on HBCUs in Maryland. Through legal advocacy, policy reform, and community engagement, the organization has addressed disparities in funding and resources that have long plagued HBCUs compared to predominantly white institutions. By highlighting the systemic challenges faced by HBCUs, such as underfunding, inadequate facilities, and limited program offerings, the Lawyer's Committee has brought attention to the barriers hindering these institutions' ability to provide quality education to black and minority students.

One of the Lawyers' Committee's notable efforts includes ongoing litigation against the state of Maryland in the *Coalition for Equity and Excellence in Maryland Higher Education v. Maryland Higher Education Commission* case. This lawsuit, initiated in 2006, challenges the state's higher education funding practices, alleging that they perpetuate segregation and inequality by systematically underfunding HBCUs (Weiner, 2021). Through this and other legal battles, the Lawyers' Committee seeks to secure fair and equitable funding policies that ensure HBCUs receive the resources they need to thrive. By advocating for HBCUs as vital engines of opportunity and social mobility, the organization aims to create a more just and inclusive educational system where all students have equal access to quality higher education, regardless of race or background.

McCleary Evans v. Maryland Highway Administration

For these reasons, judges who understand that racism is sometimes invisible are the better-qualified jurists. Consider the dissenting opinion of Judge Wynn in the case of *McCleary Evans v. Maryland Highway Administration*. With great insight and wisdom, he wrote (*McCleary-Evans v. Md. Dep't of Transp.*, 2014):

> The district court faulted McCleary–Evans for failing to allege how much control the Highway Administration employees named in the complaint "wield[ed]" over other members of the hiring committee and failing to identify the qualifications of the selected candidates. J.A. 27–28. It is simply unrealistic to expect McCleary–Evans to allege such facts without the benefit of at least some limited discovery. When we impose unrealistic expectations on plaintiffs at the pleading stage of a lawsuit, we fail to apply our "judicial experience and common sense" to the highly "context-specific task" of deciding whether to permit a lawsuit to proceed to discovery. Iqbal, 556 U.S. at 679, 129 S.Ct. 1937. At the early stages of Title VII litigation, borderline conclusory allegations may be all that is available to even the most diligent of plaintiffs. The requisite proof of the defendant's discriminatory intent is often in the exclusive control of the defendant, behind doors slammed shut by an unlawful termination.

Judge Wynn clearly understands the power dynamics of an employment relationship, racism, and classism.

Such jurists are also likely to understand why blacks with felon records are less likely to be hired than whites with felon records. An Arizona State University study showed (Decker et al., 2015):

- Both black and Hispanic men were less likely to receive a positive response from employers—including a callback or email for an interview or a job offer—compared with white men.

- Men with criminal records were more likely than women with criminal records to receive a negative response from employers.

- White men with a criminal record had more positive responses than black men with no criminal record.

White Supremacy and Authoritarianism

Understanding the influence of white supremacy and authoritarianism on judicial opinions and the broader landscape of judicial reform is imperative in confronting systemic injustices within legal systems. White supremacy, as an ideology rooted in the belief of white racial superiority, often manifests in subtle and overt biases that shape judicial decision-making. Similarly, authoritarianism, characterized by strict obedience to authority and the suppression of dissent, can impede efforts toward progressive judicial reform by reinforcing hierarchical power structures and stifling dissenting voices.

U.S. Supreme Court Dismisses Case Involving Employees Subjected to Racial Slurs

The U.S. Supreme Court had the opportunity to interpret the law with widespread ramifications over a racially hostile work environment when it considered the use of the N-word against employees. Robert Collier appealed his case to the U.S. Supreme Court. His appeal stems from his employment at Parkland Memorial Hospital in Dallas, Texas, from 2009 to 2016, culminating in his termination. Alleging discrimination, Collier filed a lawsuit asserting that he and fellow black colleagues endured disparate treatment compared to their non-black counterparts. A particularly egregious incident cited in the lawsuit involves the discovery of the N-word etched into the wall of an elevator frequently utilized by Collier and other employees to access the cafeteria—a distressing symbol of racial hostility and prejudice within the workplace (Sousou, n.d.).

His search for justice fell on deaf ears.

Chapter 6:

Judicial Reform and Systemic Bias Against People of Color

Judicial reform is critical in modern legal systems, aiming to address the inequities and inefficiencies that undermine justice. One of the most pressing concerns within this realm is the systemic bias against people of color. Historical and contemporary evidence suggests that racial minorities often face disproportionate rates of arrest, harsher sentencing, and discriminatory treatment throughout the judicial process. This bias perpetuates social and economic disparities and erodes public trust in the legal system. Addressing these deep-seated issues requires comprehensive reforms that promote fairness, accountability, and inclusivity, ensuring that justice is genuinely impartial to race and ethnicity.

The Equal Justice Committee of Maryland

Maryland established the Equal Justice Committee to address and rectify systemic inequalities within the state's judicial system, mainly focusing on the biases that affect people of color and marginalized groups. Comprising judges, attorneys, community leaders, and advocates, the committee aims to promote fairness and equity by reviewing court policies, procedures, and practices. Key initiatives include implicit bias training for judicial personnel, revising sentencing guidelines, and enhancing transparency and accountability. By engaging with affected communities and incorporating their experiences, the committee strives to create a judicial system that upholds justice and impartiality for all Maryland citizens.

Nature and Purpose

The Equal Justice Committee aims to identify and rectify systemic inequalities within the judicial system, particularly those affecting people of color and marginalized groups. Its purpose is to promote fairness, equity, and impartiality in the judiciary by reviewing and reforming court policies, procedures, and practices. The committee engages in initiatives such as providing implicit bias training for judicial personnel, revising sentencing guidelines to reduce disparities, and enhancing transparency and accountability (Equal Justice, n.d.). The committee ensures that the legal system upholds justice for all citizens through community engagement and comprehensive analysis.

Work Product

The work product of the Equal Justice Committee includes comprehensive reports and recommendations on judicial practices, revised policies and procedures aimed at reducing bias, and training programs for judicial officers and court staff (Gieszl & Ballou-Watts, 2023). These outputs encompass detailed analyses of existing disparities, proposed reforms to sentencing guidelines, and frameworks for enhanced transparency and accountability in the judiciary. Additionally, the committee produces educational materials and resources to foster community awareness and engagement, ensuring that its initiatives are informed by and responsive to the experiences of those most affected by systemic bias.

Forming a Sentencing Subcommittee

In June 2021, the Equal Justice Committee formed a specialized Sentencing Subcommittee to tackle the pervasive issue of sentencing disparities within the judicial system. This subcommittee focuses on analyzing and reforming sentencing practices that disproportionately impact people of color and other marginalized communities. Comprising legal experts, judges, researchers, and community representatives, the Sentencing Subcommittee promotes fairness and equity in sentencing decisions. Its work involves (Sentencing Subcommittee, 2021):

- rigorous data analysis

- the development of evidence-based guidelines

- the implementation of training programs for judicial officers

By addressing these critical issues, the Sentencing Subcommittee aims to ensure that sentencing within the judicial system is just, transparent, and devoid of systemic biases.

Focus Areas

The Sentencing Subcommittee of the Equal Justice Committee concentrates on several critical areas to address and mitigate sentencing disparities within the judicial system (Sentencing Subcommittee, 2021):

- **Data Analysis and Research:** The subcommittee conducts comprehensive studies to identify patterns of disparity in sentencing, collects and analyzes data on sentencing outcomes, and examines factors such as race, ethnicity, socioeconomic status, and geographic location to understand the extent and root causes of disparities.

- **Sentencing Guidelines and Policy Reform:** A key focus is reviewing and revising existing sentencing guidelines and policies. The subcommittee aims to develop evidence-based recommendations that promote consistency and fairness in sentencing decisions, ensuring these guidelines are free from racial and other biases.

- **Judicial Training and Education:** The subcommittee implements training programs for judges and court personnel to raise awareness about implicit biases and their impact on sentencing. These programs provide tools and strategies to help judicial officers make more equitable decisions, emphasizing the importance of impartiality and justice.

- **Community Engagement and Input:** Engaging with the community is essential to the subcommittee's work. It seeks to involve community members, particularly those from marginalized groups, in discussions about sentencing practices. This input helps ensure that the experiences inform reforms of those most affected by disparities.

- **Transparency and Accountability:** Promoting transparency in sentencing decisions is another focus area. The subcommittee advocates for greater public access to sentencing data and decision-making processes. This transparency helps hold the judicial system accountable and fosters public trust in its fairness and integrity.

- **Alternatives to Incarceration:** Exploring and promoting alternatives to incarceration, such as restorative justice programs and community service, is a priority. The subcommittee investigates and advocates for rehabilitative sentencing options rather than punitive ones, aiming to reduce recidivism and support reintegration into society.

The Sentencing Subcommittee strives to create a more equitable and just sentencing system that reflects the principles of fairness and equality for all individuals by addressing these focus areas.

Additional Activities

In addition to its primary focus areas, the Sentencing Subcommittee of the Equal Justice Committee engages in several supplementary activities to enhance its impact and effectiveness (Sentencing Subcommittee, 2021):

- **Stakeholder Collaboration:** The subcommittee works closely with various stakeholders, including law enforcement agencies, public defenders, prosecutors, advocacy groups, and academic institutions. This collaboration helps ensure a holistic approach to sentencing reform and fosters a shared commitment to equity.

- **Public Awareness Campaigns:** The subcommittee undertakes initiatives to educate the public about sentencing disparities and the need for reform. These campaigns aim to raise awareness, garner public support, and inform citizens about their rights and the judicial process.

- **Pilot Programs and Innovation:** Implementing and evaluating pilot programs is another critical activity. The subcommittee tests innovative sentencing practices and alternatives in select jurisdictions, assesses their outcomes, and scales successful models. These pilots often focus on restorative justice, diversion programs, and community-based sentencing options.

- **Legislative Advocacy:** The subcommittee actively supports laws and policies promoting fair sentencing practices, which involves drafting legislative proposals, giving testimony at hearings, and working with lawmakers to enact meaningful reforms.

- **Monitoring and Evaluation:** Ongoing monitoring and evaluation of sentencing reforms are essential activities. The subcommittee tracks the implementation and impact of its recommendations, using data to measure progress and make necessary adjustments. This continuous evaluation ensures that reforms are effective and sustainable.

- **Resource Development:** Developing resources such as toolkits, best practice guides, and educational materials for judicial officers, legal practitioners, and community organizations is a key activity. These resources support the consistent application of fair sentencing practices and facilitate the broader adoption of reforms.

- **Annual Reports and Publications:** The subcommittee produces annual reports and other publications to document its findings, activities, and progress. These reports provide transparency, share insights with the broader legal community, and contribute to the ongoing dialogue on sentencing reform.

- **Support for Victims and Communities:** Recognizing the impact of sentencing on victims and communities, the subcommittee advocates for and supports programs that address their needs, including victim assistance programs and initiatives that foster community healing and reconciliation.

Through these additional activities, the Sentencing Subcommittee enhances its capacity to address sentencing disparities comprehensively, ensuring that its efforts lead to systemic change and promote a fairer judicial system.

Systemic Bias in the State Courts

In April 2024, the Maryland Supreme Court expressed concerns about how state court rules can perpetuate systemic bias against people of color. One proposed rule change "...would have reminded judges and judicial employees to be mindful of implicit bias, and another that would have ended the use of certain drug convictions as an impeachment tool that could be used against witnesses" (O'Neill, 2024).

In other words, when it comes to judicial personnel, "...their decisions and the manner in which they are expressed should not reflect 'actual or implicit bias'" (O'Neill, 2024). These are judges policing judges on how not to engage in systemic racism or bias. The hard work of re-evaluating the thousands of criminal defendants already caught up in unjust verdicts and systemic bias was not mentioned.

How does the judiciary propose minorities with pending criminal cases in counties with few to no minorities on the bench will get a fair trial? We already know, based on the Emmett Till verdict, the Towhee Sparrow verdict, the Isaac Woodard verdict, the George Zimmerman verdict, the Rodney King verdict, and the recent Donald J. Trump hush money verdict, that the composition of a fair and impartial jury is the cornerstone of justice. Without a fair and impartial diverse jury, it's the same as having an Emmett Till courthouse in these jurisdictions with no recourse for litigants. Count on more Emmett Till verdicts.

Chapter 7:

The Importance of the Status Conference Establishing Deadlines

Judges schedule status conferences to determine the nature of the case better, the number of witnesses likely, the documentary evidence to expect, the complexity of the evidence if expert witnesses are likely, and the scope of the issues. It is an excellent opportunity to study whether this is a one-day, multiple-day, or multiple-week trial. Typically, in small claims matters, status conferences are not always held. The court usually assigns trial dates once the defendant is served and files their answer or intent to defend.

Attending a Status Conference

It is important to be attentive at the status conference so that lawyers can come to the status conference prepared to frame the issues for trial. Your lawyer must know how to frame the issues. For example, in a race discrimination case, which of the following applies:

- Did the employer discriminate against the charging party or plaintiff?

- Did the employer create and cultivate a racist culture, which impacted a protected class of people?

- Did the employer violate Title VII of the Civil Rights Act of 1964, as amended?

- Are there claims of wrongful discharge?

- Did the parties enter a Prayer for Jury Trial?

- What damages are sought? Are there expert witnesses?

- If this is a federal trial, will Daubert motions be filed, etc.?

In most instances, judges will ask how long the trial will take based on your estimation of witnesses and evidence presented. During the pretrial stages, defense lawyers spend billable hours on many pretrial activities, such as filing motions to dismiss on multiple grounds. Some grounds are jurisdictional, such as whether the court has subject matter or personal jurisdiction to hear the case. Some grounds are rooted in exemptions. In the landmark decision, *New York Times v. Sullivan*, the U.S. Supreme Court determined that certain litigants are public figures (Moser, 2024). As such, these litigants do not have the same protections as private individuals when defamation or libel are causes of action. Courts dismiss many defamation cases for these reasons.

Pretrial Motions

Many substantive motions to dismiss can cause an alteration to the trial schedule. For example, suppose your lawsuit combines constitutional due process or First Amendment issues, whistleblower actions, constructive discharge, and tort issues like intentional infliction of emotional distress. Some jurisdictions do not recognize torts like negligent infliction of emotional distress. Defense lawyers would promptly move to dismiss such charges not identified in a jurisdiction.

It takes months to evaluate such substantive motions to dismiss involving multiple legal challenges as outlined above.

If pretrial motions expend more than 100 hours of billable legal services, many plaintiffs and their lawyers will experience financial hardships. This is why many plaintiffs' lawyers require hefty retainers exceeding $40,000. Understanding this cost is why individual litigants should prepare to finance such litigation.

If you survive the motion to dismiss stage of litigation, be prepared for the discovery phase of litigation if permitted. If you are on a payment plan with your counsel, this stage of litigation is costly because it involves preparing interrogatories, requesting documents, and preparing for depositions. This phase may take more than 30, 60, or 90 days. This is why discussing these issues at the status conference matters.

Discovery

Things may change during the discovery phase of litigation. Sometimes, documents produced are in a foreign language. Some judges may decide it is the job of the plaintiff's lawyer to hire an interpreter to interpret this. I faced this issue as a practitioner litigating a product liability case involving defective automobile parts made in Korea. Fortunately, IT will make it easier to access such interpretation tools in 2024. But years ago, resources were not readily available.

The following is a list of other requests frequently made during the discovery phase:

- Interrogatories are written questions propounded to the opposing party seeking relevant, material, or reasonably calculated information to lead to the discovery of admissible evidence.

- Depositions are recorded statements made in an oral interview of a party or witness.

- Requests for Admission are written factual statements, which serve as a helpful tool to get admissions of facts from the opposing side. For example, "The City of Brunswick employed John Doe from June 1, 2017, to July 11, 2018." Another example is "John Doe signed the Deed to the property at 11 Elm Street in the presence of Mary Doe on September 4, 1989."

- Written Requests for Production of Documents ask for documents related to the case.

- Witness Affidavits are written statements by an individual under oath and penalty of perjury.

- Written requests order nonparties to appear as witnesses to testify, produce documents, or both. Subpoenas also obtain documents from nonparties.

Affidavits, depositions, responses to interrogatories, requests for admissions, and document requests are usually attached to these motions. They sometimes require months to evaluate fairly and impartially, especially when a plaintiff's complaint has many causes of action.

Judges usually face deciding motions to dismiss first and for summary judgment last. After ruling on the motion for summary judgment, the case will likely proceed to the trial stage if any causes of action remain standing.

Daubert Test

The Daubert decision, from the 1993 U.S. Supreme Court case *Daubert v. Merrell Dow Pharmaceuticals, Inc.*, set a new standard for admitting expert testimony in federal courts, emphasizing the judge's role as a gatekeeper to ensure the relevance and reliability of scientific evidence (Robinson, 2023-a). Replacing the older general acceptance test from *Frye v. United States*, the U.S. Supreme Court outlined criteria including testability, peer review, error rates, standards, and general acceptance to evaluate the reliability of expert testimony (Blackmun & Supreme

Court of the United States, 1992). This decision granted judges greater discretion in assessing scientific evidence and has since been extended to all forms of expert testimony, significantly shaping how courts handle and scrutinize expert contributions in legal proceedings.

Understanding if your expert witness will pass the Daubert test is also significant. There are many expert witnesses, but defense lawyers spend hundreds of billable hours trying to discredit and eliminate expert witnesses if they can (Morris, 2021). The filing of Daubert motions happens during the summary judgment phase, and they often challenge if the expert witness is a peer-reviewed and well-recognized expert.

Deadlines

Deadlines to file motions for summary judgment are usually part of scheduling orders. Some judges see these motions as a valuable tool to eliminate trials from going forward. Lawyers typically file motions for summary judgment after they have concluded discovery. Filing such motions is to stop the trial from proceeding further. Such motions first identify the legal standard and set forth whether there are genuine disputes of material facts. Affidavits, depositions, responses to interrogatories, requests for admissions, and document requests are usually attached to these motions. They sometimes require months to evaluate fairly and impartially, especially when a plaintiff's complaint has many causes of action.

Judges usually face deciding motions to dismiss first and for summary judgment last. After ruling on the motion for summary judgment, the case will likely proceed to the trial stage if any causes of action remain standing.

More deadlines may be necessary to file motions in limine and pretrial statements. Lawyers use motions in limine to prevent evidence from being heard at trial. Other deadlines include filing a pretrial statement to better understand after discovery, what witnesses are relevant, what documentary evidence is needed, if there are any stipulations, and what chances there are to resolve a case through mediation or settlement conferences.

Chapter 8:

The Importance of the Discovery

Process

Documentary evidence in a court case includes written or recorded information that helps prove or disprove facts. This evidence is critical because it provides tangible, verifiable proof that supports a party's claims or defenses. Here are some common types of documentary evidence presented in court (Documentary Evidence, n.d.):

- **Contracts and Agreements:** Written agreements outlining terms are crucial in business, employment, and property disputes.

- **Financial Records:** Bank statements, tax returns, and invoices demonstrating financial status are essential in financial disputes and fraud cases.

- **Correspondence:** Letters, emails, and texts showing agreements and relationships, pivotal in contractual disputes and harassment claims.

- **Official Records and Reports:** Government-issued documents verifying personal details and events.

- **Medical Records:** Health records detailing medical history and injuries used in personal injury and malpractice cases.

- **Employment Records:** Employment contracts and payroll records establish relevant job terms in employment disputes and discrimination cases.

- **Photographs and Videos:** Visual evidence depicting events or injuries used to corroborate facts in various cases.

- **Digital Records:** Electronic evidence from devices and social media is key in cybercrime and intellectual property cases.

- **Business Records:** Internal documents showing company operations used in corporate governance and shareholder disputes.

- **Expert Reports:** In forensic and medical evaluations, findings from specialists supporting or refuting claims are important.

Importance of Documentary Evidence

Documentary evidence is vital because it provides objective, verifiable proof that supports the factual assertions made by the parties in a case. Unlike oral testimony, which memory or perception can influence, documentary evidence is often more reliable and less susceptible to bias. Properly authenticated and relevant documentary evidence significantly strengthens a party's position, making it a cornerstone of legal proceedings.

Missing Documentary Evidence

Missing documentary evidence in a court case can severely hinder the ability to substantiate claims and provide a straightforward factual narrative, ultimately impacting the case outcome. Key documents such as contracts, financial records, correspondence, and official reports play a crucial role in establishing the terms of agreements, verifying financial transactions, and providing evidence of communications and events. In cases where such evidence is missing or incomplete, parties may struggle to support their arguments, leading to disputes over interpretations, obligations, and liability. This lack of documentary evidence can weaken legal claims, create uncertainty, and potentially delay or complicate the case resolution.

Additionally, the absence of medical records, employment records, visual evidence, digital records, business records, and expert reports can further exacerbate the challenges faced by litigants. Without these essential documents and proof, it becomes difficult to establish the extent and cause of injuries, verify employment terms and performance, corroborate witness testimony, or support claims involving specialized knowledge (Nance, 1991). As a result, parties may find it challenging to present a compelling case, leaving critical gaps in the evidence presented to the court. Ensuring the availability and completeness of documentary evidence is crucial for effectively delivering and resolving legal disputes, as it provides a foundation for building arguments, substantiating claims, and ultimately achieving a just outcome in the courtroom.

Helpful or Hurtful Documentary Evidence

In any legal proceeding, the documentary evidence presented can significantly impact the case's outcome, either helping or hurting the parties involved. Here's how different types of documentary evidence can influence the course of a case.

- **Documentary Evidence That Helps:**
    - **Strong Contracts:** Clear agreements support claims and obligations.

- o **Corroborative Financial Records:** Documents substantiate financial transactions and status.

- o **Credible Correspondence:** Written communications bolster positions and establish context.

- o **Substantive Official Records:** Government documents add credibility and verify key facts.

- **Documentary Evidence That Hurts (Scherman, 2019):**

  - o **Weak Contracts:** Ambiguous terms undermine enforcement and defense.

  - o **Inconsistent Finances:** Discrepancies raise doubts and damage credibility.

  - o **Damaging Correspondence:** Contradictory messages weaken credibility.

  - o **Disputed Official Records:** Challenges diminish the evidentiary value and require more evidence.

Discovery and Decision-Making

After discovery, parties must assess the strength of their case based on the documentary evidence gathered. Knowing when to continue or settle the case depends on various factors, including the quality and quantity of evidence, the likelihood of success at trial, the costs and risks associated with continued litigation, and the potential benefits of settling. Parties should carefully evaluate the documentary evidence, weigh the strengths and weaknesses of their case, and consider the advice of legal counsel before making an informed decision on whether to continue pursuing litigation or explore settlement options.

Violating a Court Order or Disobeying a Subpoena

Violating a court order or disobeying a subpoena to come to court or produce documents is a serious matter. You never know how gracious a judge may or may not be. You run the risk of being held in contempt of court. That may involve paying a fine or incarceration.

Chapter 9:

What Happens When Evidence Is Not Forthcoming From the Other Side

When evidence fails to materialize from the opposing party in a legal proceeding, it can profoundly affect the trajectory and outcome of the case. The absence or withholding of crucial evidence creates significant challenges for both parties, as it hampers the ability to substantiate claims, rebut arguments, and present a comprehensive factual narrative. In such situations, the party seeking the evidence may face obstacles in proving their case, while the opposing party may exploit the absence of proof to their advantage. This lack of forthcoming evidence can lead to legal maneuvers, disputes, and strategic decisions aimed at addressing the evidentiary gap and navigating the complexities of the legal process. Thus, understanding the implications of missing evidence and strategizing becomes essential for litigants and legal practitioners to pursue justice.

Destruction of Evidence

From a judge's standpoint, the destruction of evidence presents significant legal and procedural challenges. Such actions can be interpreted as obstructing the administration of justice, undermining the court's ability to ascertain the truth and fairly adjudicate disputes.

Judges expect parties to fulfill their preservation obligations, preserving relevant evidence once litigation is reasonably anticipated or commenced. Failure to do so may result in sanctions or adverse inferences against the party responsible for the destruction (Golriz, 2023). The absence of crucial evidence due to destruction can prejudice one party and unfairly advantage the other, depriving the court of essential information necessary for a fair resolution.

Upon evidence destruction coming to light, judges face the task of managing disputes over spoliation and assessing its impact on the fairness of proceedings. They must navigate legal standards and precedents, considering factors such as the intent behind the destruction and the materiality of the evidence. Judges can impose sanctions for spoliation, including adverse jury instructions, fines, or even dismissal of claims or defenses. Furthermore, dealing with allegations of evidence destruction adds complexity to case management, requiring judges to carefully balance the interests of the parties and uphold the principles of justice and due process. In essence, the destruction of evidence not only undermines the credibility and trustworthiness of the party responsible but also challenges the integrity of the legal process as a whole.

Retrieving Electronic Records

Retrieving computer records encompasses a range of methods and techniques, depending on the context and requirements of the situation. From a technical standpoint, data recovery software is vital in recovering deleted or lost files from various storage devices such as hard drives, SSDs, and memory cards. This approach is practical for recovering inadvertently deleted data or corrupted files. In legal proceedings, forensic analysis is helpful to extract and analyze digital evidence in a manner that preserves its integrity for use in court. Certified forensic examiners use specialized tools and methodologies to retrieve data from computers and digital devices, ensuring its admissibility and reliability as evidence.

Additionally, organizations often rely on backup systems to protect against data loss. Accessing and restoring data from backup copies stored on external servers, tapes, or cloud-based platforms is a standard method for retrieving computer records (Electronic Evidence, 2018). Network logs and archives maintained by ISPs, email providers, or server administrators can provide valuable information regarding online activities and communications. In legal contexts, parties may utilize legal processes such as subpoenas or court orders to compel the production of computer records from custodians or third-party service providers. Furthermore, a judge may seek data preservation orders to prevent the destruction or alteration of relevant data pending the resolution of legal disputes. Retrieving computer records requires technical expertise, legal knowledge, and procedural adherence to ensure the integrity and admissibility of the retrieved data in various contexts.

Accountability for Destroyed Evidence

The side that destroys evidence can be held accountable for their actions, particularly in legal proceedings where the integrity of evidence is crucial. When the court can prove either party intentionally or negligently destroyed that evidence, it can lead to severe consequences and sanctions. Courts can impose spoliation sanctions against parties responsible for evidence destruction, including adverse jury instructions, fines, cost-shifting, or even dismissal of claims or defenses. Additionally, courts may draw adverse inferences against the party responsible, assuming that the destroyed evidence would have been unfavorable to their case, significantly weakening their position (Solum & Marzen, 1989).

The destruction of evidence can have legal, ethical, and reputational consequences for the party involved. It may violate legal ethics and professional conduct rules, leading to disciplinary actions against attorneys responsible for the destruction. Furthermore, parties found to have engaged in evidence destruction may face civil liability for damages caused by their actions, including compensation for any harm the opposing party suffered. Overall, evidence destruction is taken seriously by the legal system, as it undermines the fairness and integrity of the judicial process, and there is an expectation that both parties fulfill their preservation obligations to ensure a level playing field for all litigants.

Chapter 10:

Mediation and Alternative Dispute

Resolution

Mediation and alternative dispute resolution (ADR) services offered by courts provide litigants with avenues to resolve their disputes outside of traditional courtroom litigation. These approaches aim to promote efficiency, cost-effectiveness, and a more collaborative resolution process while alleviating the burden on the court system. Here are some key aspects of mediation and ADR services (Lewis, 2023):

- **Mediation:** A neutral mediator facilitates communication and agreement between parties in a nonbinding, voluntary process, often used before trial.

- **Arbitration:** An impartial arbitrator hears arguments and renders a binding decision; unlike mediation, parties cede control, and a decision is akin to court judgment, voluntary or mandatory, based on court rules or agreement.

- **Benefits of ADR:** ADR services offer several advantages over traditional litigation, including:

    o **Cost Savings:** ADR typically requires fewer resources than courtroom litigation, reducing legal fees and expenses for the parties involved.

    o **Time Efficiency:** ADR processes are often quicker than litigation, allowing disputes to be resolved more promptly and reducing case backlog in the court system.

- o **Control and Flexibility:** Parties have more control over the process and outcome in ADR, enabling them to tailor solutions that better meet their needs and interests.

- o **Preservation of Relationships:** ADR encourages cooperation and communication between parties, potentially preserving relationships from the damage of adversarial litigation.

- **Types of Cases:** Courts offer ADR services for various civil disputes, including family law matters, contract disputes, personal injury claims, landlord-tenant disputes, etc. Some courts also provide specialized ADR programs for specific cases, such as small claims or probate matters.

- **Court-Connected Programs:** Many courts offer court-connected ADR programs, where trained mediators or arbitrators are provided by the court or through affiliated organizations. These programs may be available at various stages of the legal process, from pre-filing to post-judgment, and allow people to choose programs that suit the specific needs of different cases or parties.

Overall, mediation and alternative dispute resolution services offered by courts play a vital role in promoting access to justice, facilitating timely and efficient resolution of disputes, and empowering parties to actively participate in crafting solutions that meet their needs and interests.

American Arbitration Association

In American Arbitration Association (AAA) arbitration proceedings, initiating the process begins with filing a Demand for Arbitration, which outlines the nature of the dispute and the relief sought (Harmon, 2023). Here's an overview of this process and the associated costs (AAA, n.d.):

- **Filing the Demand for Arbitration:**

    o The claimant initiates arbitration by submitting a Demand for Arbitration to the AAA, which includes details about the parties, dispute, evidence, and relief sought; the AAA then notifies the respondent and provides a copy of the Demand.

- **Costs Involved:**

    o **Filing Fee:** The claimant is usually responsible for paying a filing fee to initiate the arbitration process. The filing fee amount varies depending on factors such as the size and complexity of the dispute.

    o **Administrative Fees:** Besides the filing fee, the AAA charges administrative costs for managing the arbitration proceedings. These fees include appointing arbitrators, scheduling hearings, and providing administrative support.

    o **Arbitrator Fees:** The parties are typically responsible for paying the fees and expenses of the arbitrators who hear their case. The AAA provides a schedule of arbitrator compensation based on factors such as the complexity of the case and the arbitrators' experience.

    o **Other Expenses:** Depending on the specific circumstances of the arbitration, there may be additional expenses such as hearing room rental, stenographer fees for transcribing proceedings, and travel expenses for arbitrators.

Parties involved in AAA arbitration need to review the AAA's rules and fee schedule carefully to understand their financial obligations and the procedures governing the arbitration process. Additionally, parties may consult legal counsel to navigate the arbitration proceedings effectively and protect their interests.

Judicial Arbitration and Mediation Services

Judicial Arbitration and Mediation Services (JAMS) arbitration is an alternative dispute resolution process provided by JAMS, a private organization that offers arbitration, mediation, and other ADR services (About Us, n.d.). Here's an overview of JAMS arbitration:

- **Initiating the Arbitration:**

    o The arbitration process starts when the claimant submits a request for arbitration to JAMS, which then notifies the respondent and provides them with a copy of the request.

- **Arbitrator Selection:**

    o JAMS offers a list of qualified arbitrators from which the parties can choose. If they cannot agree, JAMS appoints an experienced legal professional or subject matter expert based on the dispute and the parties' preferences.

- **Arbitration Process:**

    o In arbitration, parties present arguments, evidence, and witnesses in less formal hearings than court proceedings, with arbitrators acting as decision-makers, issuing procedural orders, ruling on motions, and rendering binding decisions based on the evidence and applicable law.

- **Costs and Fees:**

  - JAMS charges fees for arbitration services, which vary based on the dispute's size and complexity, the number of arbitrators, and the time required; the parties typically share these costs, but fee allocation may be specified in their agreement or determined by the arbitrators.

JAMS arbitration provides parties a flexible and efficient way of resolving disputes outside traditional litigation. JAMS's rules and procedures guide the process, and the parties can tailor the arbitration to their specific needs and preferences. JAMS arbitration can offer advantages such as confidentiality, expert decision-making, and expedited resolution compared to court litigation.

Chapter 11:

How Judges Weigh Evidence

Central to a judge's role is the meticulous weighing of evidence, a nuanced process that requires astute discernment and rigorous analysis. Judges must navigate a diverse array of evidentiary sources, ranging from witness testimony and documentary evidence to expert opinions and circumstantial clues, each bearing its significance and potential for influence. Through a judicious balancing act, judges meticulously assess each piece of evidence's credibility, relevance, and probative value, scrutinizing its merits and shortcomings to construct a coherent narrative that guides their ultimate determination. As custodians of justice, judges employ their expertise, discretion, and impartiality to weigh the scales of evidence with unwavering integrity, ensuring that the pursuit of truth remains paramount in the adjudicative process.

Preponderance of Evidence

The preponderance of the evidence standard requires them to weigh the evidence presented by both parties and determine which evidence is more convincing. This standard requires that the evidence favoring one side be more persuasive than the evidence favoring the other (Spears, 2007). Unlike the beyond-a-reasonable doubt standard used in criminal cases, which requires near certainty of guilt, the preponderance standard is lower and only requires that the evidence tilt slightly in favor of one party. Judges must carefully evaluate the credibility, relevance, and strength of the evidence to decide based on the greater weight of the evidence. This standard is commonly used in civil cases, including personal injury, contract disputes, and family law matters, where the goal is to determine liability or responsibility based on a balance of probabilities.

Clear and Convincing Evidence

The clear and convincing evidence standard represents a higher burden of proof than the preponderance of the evidence standard. Still, it falls short of the beyond-a-reasonable doubt standard used in criminal cases. When evaluating evidence under the clear and convincing standard, one party must persuade the judge that the evidence presented is highly probable and substantially more likely to be true than not true. This standard requires a higher degree of certainty than preponderance, but it does not require absolute certainty or proof beyond any doubt.

Judges applying the clear and convincing evidence standard must carefully assess the quality and reliability of the evidence presented by each party. They consider factors such as the credibility of witnesses, the consistency of testimony, corroborating evidence, and any other relevant factors that may impact the reliability of the evidence (Spears, 2007). The goal is to ensure that the evidence presented is sufficiently explicit, credible, and convincing to justify the court's decision to favor one party over the other.

Certain types of civil cases with high stakes, such as cases involving fraud, undue influence, termination of parental rights, or involuntary commitment, often require clear and convincing evidence. In these cases, the courts recognize the importance of protecting individuals' rights and interests by requiring a higher standard of proof before making significant decisions that could have serious consequences.

Overall, judges applying the clear and convincing evidence standard must weigh the evidence carefully and ensure that the evidence meets the heightened burden of proof required by this standard. They must be satisfied that the evidence presented is substantial, credible, and persuasive enough to justify the case's outcome in favor of the party bearing the burden of proof.

Beyond a Reasonable Doubt

The beyond-a-reasonable doubt standard represents the highest burden of proof in the legal system. Criminal cases use this standard where the government seeks to deprive individuals of their liberty or impose a significant punishment. When applying this standard, one party must convince the judge to a moral certainty that the defendant is guilty based on the evidence presented. The burden is on the prosecution to prove every element of the crime beyond a reasonable doubt, leaving no reasonable uncertainty in the judge's mind regarding the defendant's guilt.

Judges meticulously evaluate the prosecution's evidence, considering factors such as witness testimony, physical evidence, expert opinions, and other relevant information. They must assess the credibility and reliability of each piece of evidence and scrutinize the prosecution's case to ensure that it meets the beyond-a-reasonable doubt standard (Spears, 2007).

Judges also play a crucial role in instructing the jury on the meaning and application of the beyond-a-reasonable doubt standard. They guide the jury on the level of certainty required for a conviction and emphasize the importance of careful deliberation and impartial consideration of the evidence.

The beyond-a-reasonable doubt standard reflects society's fundamental commitment to the presumption of innocence and the principle that it is better to err on the side of acquitting the guilty than convicting the innocent. Judges must uphold this principle by ensuring the prosecution meets its burden of proof beyond any reasonable doubt before a defendant can be convicted and deprived of their liberty. As such, judges bear a heavy responsibility in criminal cases to safeguard individuals' rights and freedoms and uphold the justice system's integrity.

Chapter 12:

How Judges Handle Missing

Documents

In legal proceedings, judges have the formidable responsibility of adjudicating cases based on the evidence presented before them. Central to this process is the reliance on documentary evidence, which serves as a cornerstone in establishing facts, resolving disputes, and rendering just decisions. However, when crucial documents are missing or unavailable, judges face a formidable challenge that requires careful navigation and judicious consideration. In such instances, judges must employ a range of strategies and principles to address the absence of documents effectively, ensuring the integrity and fairness of the judicial process while striving to ascertain the truth and deliver equitable outcomes.

Witness Testimony and Clarifying Documentary Evidence

Witness testimony is crucial in substantiating or clarifying documentary evidence presented by parties. Here's how a judge might view this process (Williams, 2024):

- **Corroboration and Contextualization:** Witness testimony can provide corroboration for documentary evidence by confirming its authenticity, accuracy, or relevance to the case.

For example, a witness might testify that a contract accurately reflects the terms agreed upon by the parties. Additionally, witnesses can provide context to help interpret complex documents or clarify ambiguous language, ensuring that the court properly understands the documentary evidence.

- **Verification of Events:** Witness testimony can verify events or transactions documented in written records. For instance, a witness might testify to a particular event described in a contract or financial statement, adding credibility to the documentary evidence. This verification can be especially crucial in cases where there are disputes over the accuracy or integrity of the documents.

- **Resolution of Ambiguities or Contradictions:** Witnesses may testify to resolve ambiguities or contradictions in documentary evidence. For instance, if there are discrepancies between different versions of a document or conflicting interpretations of its contents, witness testimony can help clarify the true meaning or intent behind the document, aiding the court in its assessment of the evidence.

- **Credibility Assessment:** Judges assess the credibility of witnesses and the weight of their testimony about documentary evidence. The witness's demeanor, consistency, bias, and knowledge of the events in question influence the judge's evaluation. Witness testimony that aligns with documentary evidence and supports other credible evidence carries greater weight in the judge's decision-making process.

- **Completeness of the Record:** Witness testimony supplements the documentary record, providing additional information, context, or insights that may not be captured in written records alone. This comprehensive understanding of the facts enables judges to make well-informed decisions by thoroughly assessing all available evidence.

Overall, judges expect witness testimony to complement and enhance the probative value of documentary evidence, helping to establish facts, resolve disputes, and ultimately facilitate the fair and just resolution of legal disputes.

Witness Testimony and the Trier of Fact

Witness testimony plays a pivotal role in legal proceedings by assisting the trier of fact, whether a judge or a jury, in understanding the content and context of written documents presented as evidence. Here's how witness testimony aids in this process (Cooper, 2022):

- **Interpretation and Explanation:** Witnesses can provide insights into the meaning and significance of written documents, mainly if the language or terminology is technical, complex, or ambiguous. For example, in contracts or legal agreements, witnesses with relevant expertise can clarify the intent behind specific provisions or terms, helping the trier of fact to understand the document's legal implications.

- **Corroboration of Authenticity:** Witnesses may testify to the authenticity and origin of written documents, confirming their legitimacy and reliability. By attesting to the circumstances under which the documents were created, witnessed, or maintained, witnesses add credibility to the documentary evidence and help establish its trustworthiness in the eyes of the trier of fact.

- **Verification of Events:** Witness testimony can corroborate events or transactions documented in written records, providing firsthand accounts of the occurrences described in the documents. This verification adds weight to the documentary evidence by confirming its alignment with the facts witnessed by individuals with direct knowledge of the events in question.

- **Clarification of Intent:** Witnesses can illuminate the intent or purpose behind written communications, such as letters, emails, or memos. By offering context or background information, witnesses help the trier of fact understand the motivations, intentions, or circumstances surrounding the creation or transmission of the documents, thereby facilitating a more informed assessment of their relevance and significance to the case.

- **Resolution of Discrepancies:** Witness testimony may help resolve discrepancies or inconsistencies between different versions of written documents or conflicting interpretations of their contents. By providing additional information or explanations, witnesses assist the trier of fact in reconciling conflicting evidence and arriving at a coherent understanding of the facts.

Overall, witness testimony is a valuable complement to written documents, enriching the trier of fact's understanding of the evidence presented and enabling a more comprehensive and nuanced evaluation of the case. Witnesses play a vital role in elucidating written documents' content, context, and implications by offering firsthand accounts, insights, and explanations, thereby facilitating the pursuit of truth and justice in the adjudicative process.

Chapter 13:

Jury or Bench Trial

The choice between a jury trial and a bench trial is a critical decision that can significantly impact the proceedings and outcome of a case. While a bench trial, where the judge serves as the sole fact-finder, offers the advantages of legal expertise and efficiency, a jury trial brings the benefits of community involvement, diverse perspectives, and shared responsibility. Each option presents unique considerations regarding fairness, public perception, and the nature of the case. Judges effectively navigate the judicial process by understanding the nuances and implications of both types of trials, ensuring that they serve justice best suited to each case's specific circumstances.

Choosing a Jury Trial

Choosing a jury trial can offer several benefits, including ensuring community representation, enhancing public confidence in the legal system, and distributing decision-making responsibility, especially in complex or high-profile cases. Juries provide diverse perspectives and common sense judgments, which are valuable in assessing evidence and witness credibility (Jury Trial, 2023). Additionally, a jury trial can appear procedurally fairer in cases of significant public interest or controversy, as it involves citizens directly in the justice process and reinforces the transparency and legitimacy of the verdict.

Beware of the disadvantages of choosing a jury trial. Many citizens culturally condition themselves to undervalue testimony from certain minorities. Unless a jury member has experienced discrimination, they may not reach a decision that an employer engaged in race discrimination or ethnic discrimination, even when there is clear evidence of differential treatment. Some jurors form opinions about people's dress, speech, use of slang, or treatment of others. All eyes are usually on the parties. If they wear too much designer clothing, the jury may not want to render a verdict with a sizable award of money, especially if they themselves dress modestly and rarely wear designer clothing.

Choosing a Bench Trial

Bench trials are generally more efficient, avoiding the time-consuming process of jury selection and deliberation and allowing for quicker resolutions. Judges bring legal expertise and an objective approach to decision-making, which is beneficial in complex cases involving intricate legal issues or technical details (Bench Trial, 2022). Their ability to focus solely on the law and evidence without the influence of emotions ensures more predictable and consistent outcomes. Additionally, bench trials can offer greater privacy, reducing public and media scrutiny in sensitive cases. These factors make bench trials a preferred option in certain judicial situations.

Pathway to the Federal Bench

To get a case heard on the federal bench, you start by filing a complaint in a federal district court. This court has original jurisdiction over most federal cases. The process begins with serving the defendant and exchanging pleadings, followed by the discovery phase, where both parties gather evidence. If the case isn't dismissed or settled, it proceeds to trial, where a judge or jury delivers a verdict based on the presented evidence.

If either party is dissatisfied with the district court's decision, they can appeal to the U.S. Court of Appeals, which involves submitting briefs and potentially participating in oral arguments. The appellate court reviews the case for legal errors and makes a decision that might affirm, reverse, or remand the case. You can appeal further to the U.S. Supreme Court by petitioning for a writ of *certiorari* (United States Courts, n.d.). The Supreme Court reviews the case and issues a final decision if granted. This multistep process thoroughly examines federal cases at multiple judicial levels.

Trial Events

At trial, the following sequence of events typically occurs, whether it's a jury or bench trial:

- **Jury Selection (if applicable):** For a jury trial, the process starts by selecting a jury through voir dire, where attorneys question potential jurors to ensure impartiality.

- **Opening Statements:** Both the prosecution (or plaintiff in civil cases) and the defense present their opening statements, outlining their case and what they aim to prove.

- **Presentation of Evidence:**

  o **Prosecution's Case:** The side bringing the case presents its evidence first, calling witnesses to testify and introducing physical evidence. Each witness is subject to direct examination by the presenting party and cross-examination by the opposing party.

  o **Defense's Case:** After the prosecution rests, the defense presents its case, following the same process of direct and cross-examining witnesses.

- **Rebuttal and Surrebuttal:** The prosecution may present rebuttal evidence to counter the defense's arguments. The defense may then offer surrebuttal evidence to address the rebuttal.

- **Closing Arguments:** Both sides summarize their cases, persuading the judge or jury to favor their arguments based on the evidence presented.

- **Jury Instructions (if applicable):** In a jury trial, the judge provides the jury with legal standards and guidelines to follow when deliberating and reaching a verdict.

- **Deliberation and Verdict:**

  - **Jury Deliberation:** The jury retires to deliberate in private, discussing the case and the evidence to reach a verdict.

  - **Bench Trial Decision:** In a bench trial, the judge considers the evidence and decides.

- **Verdict Announcement:** The jury (or judge in a bench trial) announces the verdict, determining whether the defendant is guilty or not guilty in a criminal trial or liable in a civil trial.

- **Post-Trial Motions:** Following the verdict, either party may file post-trial motions, such as a motion for a new trial or a motion for judgment notwithstanding the verdict.

- **Sentencing or Judgment:** In a criminal trial, the judge will later impose a sentence if the verdict is guilty. In a civil trial, the judge will issue a judgment determining any awards for damages or other remedies.

These steps ensure a structured and fair trial process, allowing both sides to present their case and ensuring justice is administered based on the evidence and legal principles.

Chapter 14:

The Verdict

In the complex tapestry of the legal system, verdicts stand as the definitive outcomes of court cases, representing the culmination of exhaustive legal proceedings and deliberations. These determinations, whether rendered by a jury or a judge in a bench trial, hold profound significance, shaping the lives of those involved and serving as benchmarks of justice. Verdicts are not merely conclusions but reflections of the application of law to evidence, embodying the principles of fairness, impartiality, and the rule of law (Robinson, 2023-b). In family law, verdicts are outcomes that decide the custody of your children, such as whether you get joint custody, shared custody, or full custody. Verdicts decide on child support and alimony. Verdicts determine the distribution of marital assets.

Verdicts are outcomes juries decide. It may be as simple as whether the defendant in a civil case is liable or not liable. It may be more complex based on the number of issues presented in a case.

In other civil matters, such as shareholder derivative suits, verdicts decide if a minority shareholder's objections will prevail over majority shareholders.

Only judges possess the authority to decide on certain equity matters.

In declaratory judgment, courts determine the recognition of specific causes of action under a state's law or, if there is no supportive case law, whether they should declare a particular law.

From criminal trials where guilt or innocence hangs in the balance to civil cases where liability and compensation are at stake, verdicts wield the power to bring closure, deliver accountability, and uphold the integrity of the legal system. As the climax of the trial process, verdicts illuminate the essence of justice and the resilience of the legal framework in resolving disputes and adjudicating matters of profound importance to individuals, communities, and society as a whole.

After the Verdict

The trial process does not necessarily conclude with the verdict due to several subsequent legal steps that can influence the outcome. These post-verdict procedures include (ABA, 2021):

- **Post-Trial Motions:** After rendering a verdict, the losing party often files post-trial motions, such as a motion for a new trial or a motion for judgment notwithstanding the verdict. These motions argue that there were legal errors during the trial or that the evidence does not support the jury's decision.

- **Sentencing in Criminal Trials:** A guilty verdict leads to a separate sentencing phase in criminal cases. The judge considers various factors, such as the severity of the crime, the defendant's criminal history, and any mitigating or aggravating circumstances, before determining the appropriate sentence.

- **Appeals:** Both parties have the right to appeal the verdict. The appellate process involves reviewing the trial court's proceedings for legal errors that may have affected the outcome. Appeals courts evaluate whether the law was applied correctly and the trial was fair, but they do not retry cases.

- **Enforcement of Judgments in Civil Cases:** Winning a civil case results in a judgment for damages or other remedies, but enforcing this judgment can be complex. The losing party may resist payment or compliance, requiring additional legal action to enforce the court's order.

- **Post-Conviction Relief:** In criminal cases, defendants may seek post-conviction relief through various motions and petitions, such as habeas corpus, claiming new evidence, ineffective assistance of counsel, or other violations of their rights.

- **Parole and Probation:** Parole or probation often involves ongoing legal supervision and carries the potential for legal action if there is a violation of the terms. These post-sentencing phases can significantly impact the defendant's life and require continuous legal oversight.

- **Settlements and Negotiations:** After a verdict, parties in civil cases might negotiate settlements to avoid prolonged legal battles, which can involve renegotiating the payment terms or agreeing on a reduced amount.

- **Public and Professional Repercussions:** The parties involved may face ongoing professional or public consequences, such as disciplinary actions against attorneys, regulatory reviews, or broader social and reputational impacts.

These post-verdict steps ensure that the judicial process thoroughly addresses all aspects of the case, safeguards legal rights, and enforces the court's decisions, contributing to the overall pursuit of justice.

Chapter 15:

Post-Judgment Motions

Post-judgment motions are critical procedural tools in the judicial process, allowing parties to seek redress or correction after rendering a verdict. These motions, which can include motions for a new trial, motions for judgment notwithstanding the verdict (JNOV), and motions to amend or alter the judgment, allow for judicial review of potential errors, ensure the fairness of the trial, and uphold the integrity of the legal system. Post-judgment motions are vital in pursuing accurate and equitable litigation outcomes by providing a mechanism to address perceived injustices or procedural flaws.

Motion for JNOV

A motion for JNOV is a legal request made by a party in a trial, typically after a jury has returned a verdict. The motion asks the court to set aside the jury's verdict and enter a different judgment. The basis for this motion is that the evidence did not support the jury's verdict or was contrary to the law.

Purpose and Basis

A motion for JNOV primarily challenges a jury's findings because no reasonable jury could have reached the given verdict based on the evidence presented (ABA, 2019). The moving party argues that the verdict lacks sufficient evidence or contradicts applicable legal principles. The standard for granting a JNOV is stringent, requiring the court to determine that no reasonable jury could have arrived at the verdict, indicating that the evidence overwhelmingly supports one side, making the jury's decision a clear error.

Procedure and Grounds for JNOV

Typically, parties file a motion for JNOV after the jury delivers its verdict but before formally entering judgment, often alongside or with a motion for a new trial. Depending on jurisdictional rules, it must be filed within a specific time frame, usually a few days to a few weeks after the verdict. Grounds for a JNOV encompass insufficient evidence, where the evidence fails to support the jury's findings even when viewed favorably for the non-moving party, and legal error, where the jury's verdict stems from the incorrect application of the law, such as erroneous jury instructions or misinterpretation of legal principles.

Court's Consideration

When considering a motion for JNOV, the court reviews all evidence in the light most favorable to the non-moving party without weighing the evidence or assessing witness credibility. The judge's task is to determine if there is a legally sufficient basis for a reasonable jury to reach the verdict. Additionally, the court applies the relevant legal standards to the facts, ensuring that the jury's application of the law was reasonable and correctly interpreted based on the evidence presented.

Outcomes

If the court grants a motion for JNOV, it overturns the jury's verdict and enters a judgment in favor of the moving party, effectively nullifying the jury's decision. If the court denies the motion, it affirms the jury's verdict and enters judgment accordingly. The losing party can appeal the decision on a JNOV. If granted, the non-moving party can appeal to reinstate the jury's verdict, while if denied, the moving party can appeal, arguing that the verdict should have been overturned.

Strategic Considerations

A motion for JNOV is a crucial post-verdict strategy for parties challenging the jury's verdict as erroneous. It provides an additional judicial review layer and can precede an appeal. Often filed alongside motions for a new trial, a JNOV seeks to overturn the verdict. In contrast, a new trial motion aims to retry the case due to procedural errors, new evidence, or other issues affecting trial fairness.

A JNOV challenges the sufficiency of evidence supporting the jury's verdict, ensuring it aligns with the law and the evidence presented.

Motion for Reconsideration

Motions for reconsideration are legal requests made to a court by a party asking to review and alter a court's prior decision. Litigants can file these motions in various contexts, including after a judgment or an interim order, and they play a crucial role in ensuring judicial decisions are fair, correct, and just.

Purpose and Grounds

A motion for reconsideration enables a court to rectify its errors, address new evidence, or entertain fresh legal arguments not previously presented, ensuring the decision accurately reflects the law and facts. Grounds for such a motion include correcting clear errors of law or fact in the original decision, presenting new evidence that could substantially impact the outcome and was unavailable initially, recognizing relevant changes in the law affecting the decision, and preventing manifest injustices that would arise if the original decision were left unaltered (Motion for Reconsideration, 2021).

Procedure

The filing of a motion for reconsideration involves adhering to specific procedural requirements. The timing varies depending on jurisdiction but commonly falls within a short period following the decision, typically ranging from 10 to 30 days. The party must submit this motion to the court that issued the original decision. It typically consists of a written memorandum detailing the reasons for reconsideration, supported by pertinent legal arguments and, if applicable, newly presented evidence. Essential content requirements include:

- explicitly stating the grounds for reconsideration

- identifying specific errors or introducing new evidence

- articulating how these elements justify a different outcome

Consideration by the Court

In reviewing a motion for reconsideration, the court exercises discretion to decide whether to grant it, assessing if there are compelling reasons warranting a revisit to the decision. Typically, the court confines the scope of reconsideration to the issues specifically raised in the motion, refraining from re-arguing matters already decided unless a clear basis exists for reconsideration. This approach ensures that the reconsideration process addresses the grounds presented in the motion, promoting efficiency and fairness in judicial proceedings.

Outcomes

When a court grants a motion for reconsideration, it reserves the right to amend or reverse its initial decision in light of new arguments or evidence presented, which may lead to a modified judgment or order that aligns more accurately with the correct application of the law. Conversely, if the court denies the motion, the original decision remains unchanged. However, this denial can often be appealed to a higher court, provided that the circumstances and procedural rules permit such an appeal.

Strategic Considerations

Filing a motion for reconsideration necessitates adherence to timely submission and ensuring that the grounds are compelling and supported by legal precedent and evidence. Mere disagreement with the court's decision isn't adequate for reconsideration. Such motions can form part of a broader post-judgment strategy, possibly accompanied by motions like those for a new trial or an appeal, to exhaust all avenues for challenging the decision. It's vital to recognize jurisdictional variations, as different regions have specific rules and standards for such motions, necessitating familiarity with local court procedures for effective drafting and filing.

Motions for reconsideration serve as crucial legal tools, providing parties with a means to rectify judicial errors, introduce new evidence, and uphold justice. They permit courts to reassess decisions in light of new information or errors, thereby fostering fairness and precision in the legal process. Understanding their purpose, procedure, and strategic implications is imperative for effective legal advocacy.

Motion for a New Trial

A motion for a new trial is a legal request made to a court seeking to overturn or set aside the outcome of a trial and have the case retried. These motions are typically filed after a verdict has been reached but before the judgment becomes final.

Purpose and Grounds

The purpose of a motion for a new trial is to address errors or irregularities that occurred during the trial, potentially impacting the fairness of the outcome (ABA, 2019). This legal remedy allows parties to present new evidence, challenge jury instructions, or address other trial errors that warrant a retrial. Grounds for such a motion include demonstrating legal errors by the court, such as incorrect jury instructions or admission of inadmissible evidence; proving misconduct by jurors, attorneys, or the judge that compromised trial fairness; presenting new evidence discovered after the trial; and showing that errors during the trial prejudiced the party's rights, resulting in an unjust verdict.

Procedure

Filing a motion for a new trial involves adherence to specific procedural requirements. The timing for submission varies across jurisdictions but generally falls within a designated period following the verdict, typically ranging from a few days to a few weeks. This motion must be submitted to the court overseeing the trial and served on all involved parties. It typically includes a written memorandum delineating the grounds for the new trial, supported by legal arguments and, if applicable, new evidence. Essential content requirements entail specifying the grounds for the new trial, providing detailed explanations and evidence supporting these grounds, and addressing each alleged error or irregularity separately while elucidating why it necessitates a retrial.

Consideration by the Court

When reviewing a motion for a new trial, the court assesses the grounds presented to determine if they meet the legal standard for granting such a request. Courts typically have discretion in deciding whether to grant a new trial, where they weigh the significance of the errors or irregularities alleged in the motion and their impact on the fairness of the trial. This discretionary power allows courts to consider the overall fairness of the proceedings and the potential consequences of granting or denying the motion.

Outcomes

When a court grants a motion for a new trial, it overturns the previous verdict. It mandates a case retrial, allowing the parties to present their arguments anew before a different jury or judge. Conversely, if the court denies the motion, the original verdict remains, and the judgment becomes final. However, the denial of a motion for a new trial typically can be appealed to a higher court, allowing parties to seek further review of the trial court's decision.

Strategic Considerations

Strategic timing is crucial when filing a motion for a new trial, ensuring adherence to procedural deadlines and enhancing the likelihood of success. It's imperative to present compelling evidence and persuasive legal arguments supporting the grounds for a retrial to persuade the court of its necessity. In the event of denial, parties can appeal the decision to a higher court, seeking a review of the trial court's ruling.

A motion for a new trial is a significant post-trial legal recourse, enabling parties to contest trial outcomes based on errors or irregularities during the proceedings. Mastery of the grounds, procedure, and strategic considerations surrounding these motions is essential for effective legal advocacy.

Collecting on Judgment

Collecting on a judgment may require additional proceedings, especially if the defendant is not forthcoming about their assets. Sometimes, lawyers hire private investigators to determine better if pursuing the case is worth it. When choosing to sue someone, always consider the person's ability to pay the debt and the likelihood the individual may file for bankruptcy. Even if they file for bankruptcy, you still may file a claim in the bankruptcy case.

The methods available for collecting on a judgment vary depending on the jurisdiction and the case's specific circumstances. Common methods of enforcement include (Trapp et al., 2021):

- **Wage Garnishment:** The court orders the judgment debtor's employer to withhold a portion of the debtor's wages to satisfy the debt.

- **Bank Levy:** The judgment creditor can obtain a court order to freeze the judgment debtor's bank account and seize funds to satisfy the debt.

- **Property Lien:** A lien can be placed on the judgment debtor's real property (such as a house or land) or personal property (such as a car) to secure payment of the debt. If the debtor sells the property, the creditor may receive payment from the proceeds.

- **Asset Seizure:** In some cases, the court may authorize the seizure of the judgment debtor's assets, such as vehicles or valuable personal property, to satisfy the debt.

- **Assignment Orders:** This involves directing a third party who owes money to the judgment debtor, such as a bank or tenant, to pay the funds directly to the judgment creditor instead.

However, collecting on a judgment can be challenging, especially if the judgment debtor lacks sufficient assets or income to satisfy the debt. In such cases, the judgment creditor may need to explore alternative options, such as negotiating a payment plan with the debtor or seeking assistance from a collections agency.

Judgment creditors need to be aware of the legal procedures and limitations governing the collection process in their jurisdiction. Consulting with an attorney experienced in debt collection can provide valuable guidance and assistance in navigating the complexities of enforcing a judgment.

Chapter 16:

The Decision to Appeal

Deciding whether or not to appeal a case involves carefully considering various factors, each of which plays a crucial role in determining the likelihood of success and the potential consequences of pursuing an appeal.

The Right to Appeal

The right to appeal is a crucial element of the judicial system, allowing individuals to challenge lower court decisions and seek a fair and just outcome. It ensures oversight by higher courts, which review legal and procedural errors to prevent miscarriages of justice. The appellate process typically involves filing a notice of appeal, submitting written briefs, and possibly presenting oral arguments. Appellate courts then issue decisions that may affirm, reverse, modify, or remand the case. Appeals focus on errors of law, procedural mistakes, and occasionally factual findings, with different standards of review applied. This process protects individual rights, promotes judicial accountability, and helps develop and clarify legal precedents.

Death Penalty Cases

The right to appeal in death penalty cases is crucial for ensuring a thorough review of convictions and sentences to prevent miscarriages of justice. This process includes mandatory automatic appeals in most jurisdictions, where a higher court, often the state's supreme court, reviews the case to ensure fair trial procedures, correct application of law, and sufficient evidence. Following direct appeals, defendants can seek state post-conviction relief to introduce new evidence or claims of ineffective counsel. They can file federal habeas corpus petitions for constitutional reviews if denied, though strict procedural rules constrain these. Successive petitions are rare and require exceptional circumstances. As a final option, defendants can request clemency from executive authorities, seeking mercy when legal avenues are exhausted.

The multilayered appellate process aims to safeguard against wrongful convictions and ensure the reasonable application of the death penalty.

Strength of Legal Issues

Assessing the strength of legal issues raised in a case is pivotal in determining the viability of an appeal. This process involves a comprehensive analysis of potential legal errors during trial proceedings, such as misinterpretations of law, erroneous jury instructions, or constitutional violations, which could support a successful appeal. Strong legal arguments are firmly rooted in precedent, statutes, and legal principles, where precedent refers to prior court decisions establishing relevant legal principles. Well-reasoned arguments aligning with established legal precedents are more persuasive to appellate courts. Additionally, legal issues directly implicating statutory or constitutional rights undergo heightened scrutiny on appeal. Therefore, articulating compelling legal arguments supported by relevant authority increases the chances of success. Ultimately, the strength of legal issues raised significantly influences the appellate court's decision on whether to reverse or affirm the lower court's ruling.

Appellate Review Standards

Understanding appellate review standards is crucial for parties considering an appeal. Appellate courts apply different standards to various issues raised on appeal, impacting the likelihood of success. De novo review, common for questions of law, allows appellate courts to independently assess legal issues without deferring to the lower court's decision and offers parties an opportunity to challenge legal interpretations or rulings (Hilotin-Lee, 2024). Conversely, deferential review typically applies to factual findings, where appellate courts defer to the trial court unless conclusions are erroneous or unsupported by evidence. Recognizing these standards enables parties to assess argument strength and likelihood of success. For issues subject to de novo review, presenting persuasive legal arguments supported by precedent is crucial. Demonstrating trial court errors or lack of evidence is vital for factual matters. Understanding these standards helps parties tailor appellate arguments for maximum success.

Evidence and Record

Evaluating trial evidence and reviewing the appellate record is crucial in determining appeal viability. Appellate courts often defer to trial court factual findings due to their advantage in assessing evidence. Thus, showing clear errors in factual determinations or evidentiary rulings is key for a successful appeal, which involves meticulously reviewing trial transcripts, exhibits, and records to identify discrepancies. If the appellate court finds trial errors, it may reverse the lower court's decision.

Raising objections and making timely motions ensures that errors are adequately preserved for appellate review, thereby preserving issues for appeal. A comprehensive record strengthens appeal chances. Therefore, parties must carefully evaluate trial evidence and review records to identify errors warranting appellate intervention.

Procedural Requirements

Following procedural requirements is crucial when filing an appeal to preserve the appellate rights of the parties. Jurisdictions govern appellate procedures with specific rules and deadlines, and failure to comply can result in severe consequences, including appeal dismissal. Understanding procedural intricacies and ensuring strict compliance is vital for a successful appeal. Critical among these requirements is adherence to filing deadlines, with appellate courts imposing strict time limits, typically from the entry of the lower court's final judgment or order. Missing these deadlines can lead to dismissal, depriving the appellant of appellate review.

Additionally, appellate rules dictate formatting, content, and service requirements for briefs, motions, and filings. Failure to comply can result in rejection or dismissal, further risking the appeal's success. Compliance also involves following appellate court rules on jurisdiction, venue, filing fees, and party identification, as deviations may raise jurisdictional issues or procedural hurdles. Appellate proceedings often entail complex procedural matters, requiring familiarity to impact the appeal outcome significantly. Thus, adherence to procedural requirements demands a thorough understanding of rules, deadlines, and intricacies, ensuring compliance to maximize appeal success and avoid potential dismissal or adverse outcomes.

Potential Outcomes

Assessing potential outcomes of an appeal is vital for parties contemplating appellate review. It involves examining potential rulings the appellate court could issue and analyzing their impact on the case. One outcome is affirmance, where the lower court's decision stands, resulting in no relief for the appellant and potentially added costs. Conversely, reversal grants relief sought by the appellant, possibly leading to a new trial or modified decision. However, even if the appellate court reverses the lower court's decision, it may remand the case for further proceedings. A mixed ruling affirms some aspects while reversing or remanding others, requiring careful consideration and possibly more litigation. Dismissal on procedural grounds means no substantive resolution. A realistic evaluation, considering legal strength, likelihood of success, costs, and impact, is crucial for an informed decision. By assessing potential outcomes, parties can make strategic choices aligning with their objectives to maximize favorable results.

Costs and Resources

Most courts allow truly poor litigants to petition to waive the filing fees. But the courts want access to your financial statements, which may turn off many litigants struggling financially.

Assessing the costs and resources required for an appeal is crucial for parties weighing appellate review. Appeals are complex, lengthy, and costly, involving significant financial investments and resource allocation. Attorney fees constitute a primary cost, reflecting the specialized expertise and preparation needed for appellate advocacy.

For example, the printing costs of preparing an appellate brief usually are around $2,500 to $5,000. The filing fee for a notice of appeal is usually $400 in the U.S. Courts of Appeal in the various circuits (Williams, 2023). The U.S. Supreme Court receives between 5,000 and 7,000 cases annually and accepts only a fraction of these cases for oral arguments after a petition for a writ of certiorari is granted (Supreme Court, n.d.). Litigants file petitions for writ of certiorari when statutes do not allow an appeal of rights, which means that the highest court in the United States hears roughly 1% and 3% of cases the average citizen brings. This is not justice.

Client Objectives

Understanding the client's goals and objectives is paramount for effective representation in appellate matters. Each client brings unique considerations that significantly influence the decision to pursue an appeal. Therefore, attorneys must thoroughly communicate with their clients to grasp their objectives and discuss potential outcomes, including various rulings and implications for the case. By comprehensively understanding potential benefits and risks, attorneys empower clients to make informed decisions. Aligning appellate strategy with the client's interests ensures the effective pursuit of objectives. When developing a plan, attorneys consider desired outcomes, risk tolerance, timelines, and budgets. For example, clients prioritizing swift resolutions may prefer settlements, while those seeking legal rights vindication may pursue appeals vigorously. Maintaining open communication throughout the appellate process is vital. Attorneys keep clients informed, discuss strategic decisions, and address concerns to provide tailored representation. Understanding and aligning with client objectives are fundamental to appellate success and client satisfaction.

Precedent and Case Law

Researching relevant precedents and case law is a cornerstone of appellate practice and is crucial for understanding the legal context surrounding issues raised on appeal. Precedent, established by prior court decisions, guides legal interpretation and application (ABA, 2022). By studying similar cases, attorneys gain insights into relevant legal principles, arguments, and reasoning. This research helps anticipate how the appellate court may rule on appeal issues, allowing attorneys to gauge argument strengths and tailor strategies accordingly. Furthermore, it identifies favorable authorities supporting the client's position and prepares attorneys to address adverse precedents.

Anticipating and responding to counterarguments is facilitated by thorough research, enabling effective advocacy. Overall, comprehensive legal research strengthens arguments and enhances the likelihood of appellate success, ensuring favorable outcomes for clients.

Deciding whether to appeal a case involves weighing these factors and considering the merits of the appeal in light of the case's specific circumstances. It requires a thorough understanding of the law, the appellate process, and the potential risks and benefits of pursuing an appeal.

Chapter 17:

How to Finance Protracted

Litigation

The legal system often fails to serve people experiencing poverty equitably. Designed with a framework that presumes equal access and resources, it inadvertently marginalizes those without financial means. The high costs associated with legal representation, court fees, and the protracted nature of litigation create insurmountable barriers for the economically disadvantaged. Consequently, a comprehensive plan is essential to finance hundreds of hours of extended legal battles, ensuring that justice is not a privilege of the wealthy but a right accessible to all. Addressing this disparity is crucial for maintaining the integrity and fairness of the legal system.

Organizations that Provide Legal Services and Resources

In addition to traditional legal aid organizations, several other entities provide legal services or resources to those in need, often focusing on specific demographics or legal issues. These organizations help bridge the gap for individuals who may not qualify for legal aid but still require assistance navigating the legal system (Find A Lawyer, 2024):

- **Advocacy Groups:** Organizations like the National Immigration Law Center and the Equal Justice Initiative focus on issues like immigration rights and criminal justice reform. They provide legal representation, advocacy, and education to support vulnerable populations.

- **Community Legal Clinics:** Universities and law schools often run legal clinics offering free or low-cost legal services to the community. These clinics, staffed by law students under the supervision of experienced attorneys, assist in areas such as consumer rights, housing, and family law.

- **Court-Based Self-Help Centers:** Many courts have established self-help centers to assist individuals representing themselves. These centers provide resources such as legal forms, instructional guides, and sometimes limited advice from volunteer attorneys.

- **Legal Hotlines:** Some organizations operate legal hotlines, providing immediate legal advice and information over the phone. Examples include the Legal Information Referral Service and various state-specific hotlines.

- **Nonprofit Organizations:** The American Civil Liberties Union and the Southern Poverty Law Center actively provide legal representation and advocacy when a violation of rights occurs. These organizations often engage in impact litigation to bring about broader societal changes.

- **Online Legal Resources:** Platforms like LegalZoom and Rocket Lawyer offer affordable legal documents and limited attorney consultations. While not a substitute for full legal representation, these services can help individuals handle simpler legal matters independently.

- **Pro Bono Networks:** Many bar associations and law firms have established pro bono programs where attorneys volunteer their time and expertise. Examples include the Pro Bono Institute and local bar associations' pro bono committees.

These networks often focus on cases involving civil rights, housing, immigration, and family law.

These organizations and resources are crucial in ensuring more people have access to legal support, addressing gaps that traditional legal aid may not cover. By leveraging the expertise and resources of diverse entities, the legal system can become more accessible and equitable for all individuals, regardless of their financial status.

Grant Funding Resources

Grant funding can be a crucial resource for organizations striving to provide legal services to underserved populations. Several entities, including the American Funding Group and other foundations, offer grant opportunities to support legal aid initiatives and related causes. Here's an overview of some key organizations that provide such funding:

- **The American Bar Association (ABA) Fund for Justice and Education:** The ABA Fund for Justice and Education supports many public service and education programs. Through grants, it funds projects that improve access to justice, enhance the quality of legal services, and promote public understanding of the law (ABA, n.d.-a).

- **The American Funding Group:** Specializing in grant funding, it helps nonprofit organizations secure financial resources to support their missions. They offer assistance in identifying appropriate grants and navigating the application process. Their focus spans various sectors, including legal services, ensuring organizations can access the necessary funding to deliver critical legal support.

- **The Ford Foundation:** The Ford Foundation supports initiatives that promote social justice and reduce inequality.

Their grants fund organizations that work on criminal justice reform, civil rights, and access to legal services for disadvantaged populations (Ford Foundation, n.d.).

- **Legal Services Corporation (LSC):** The LSC is a nonprofit corporation established by Congress to fund legal aid programs across the United States. It grants organizations that offer civil legal assistance to low-income individuals (LSC, n.d.). The LSC is a significant funder of legal aid programs, helping them provide essential services such as representation in housing, consumer, family, and employment law cases.

- **The NAACP Legal Defense Fund (LDF):** The NAACP LDF provides grant funding resources to support litigation efforts to combat racial discrimination and advance civil rights causes, fostering a more just and equitable society (LDF, n.d.).

- **Washington Lawyers' Committee for Civil Rights:** The Washington Lawyers' Committee for Civil Rights offers grant funding resources to support litigation, advocacy, and outreach efforts aimed at addressing civil rights issues and promoting social justice in the Washington, D.C., metropolitan area (Washington Lawyers' Committee, n.d.).

These funding organizations are vital in enabling legal service providers to expand their reach and enhance their impact. By securing grant funding, legal aid organizations can better support their missions, ensuring that more individuals receive the legal assistance they need, regardless of their financial circumstances.

Payment Plans With Law Firms

Navigating the high costs of legal services can be challenging, particularly for individuals with limited financial resources. To make legal representation more accessible, many law firms offer flexible payment plans. Here are several common strategies and considerations for making payment plans with law firms (Livni, 2019):

- **Contingency Fee Basis:** In cases like personal injury claims, some law firms work on a contingency fee basis, where the client pays a percentage of the settlement or judgment as the lawyer's fee. If the client does not win the case, they may not owe any attorney fees, making legal representation more accessible to clients who cannot afford upfront costs.

- **Credit and Financing Options:** Law firms might partner with financing companies to offer loans or credit lines specifically for legal fees. Clients can finance their legal expenses and repay over time, often with interest. This option provides immediate access to funds, which can be crucial for urgent legal matters.

- **Flat Fee Arrangements:** Law firms might offer a flat fee arrangement for certain cases, particularly those that are more predictable in scope and involve agreeing on a price for the entire case, which you can pay in installments. This approach provides clients with clear cost expectations and manageable payment schedules.

- **Hourly Rate Payment Plans:** Law firms may agree to spread out payments over time based on an hourly rate. Clients can pay in installments as services are rendered rather than a lump sum upfront, making it easier for clients to manage legal expenses gradually.

- **Legal Insurance Plans:** Some clients may have access to legal insurance plans through their employers or professional associations. These plans often cover specific legal fees or provide discounts, reducing the financial burden on clients.

- **Payment Plan Agreements:** Formal payment plan agreements between the client and the law firm outline the payment terms, including the total amount due, the payment schedule, and any interest or late fees. Clear agreements help prevent misunderstandings and ensure both parties are on the same page.

- **Retainer Agreements:** Some law firms require a retainer fee, an upfront payment, to secure their services. Firms may allow the retainer to be paid in installments to accommodate clients. The retainer is typically held in a trust account and covers ongoing legal fees.

- **Sliding Scale Fees:** Some law firms adjust their fees based on the client's ability to pay. Sliding scale fees are typically based on the client's income and financial situation, ensuring that lower-income clients can still access necessary legal services.

By offering flexible payment plans, law firms can make their services more accessible, allowing clients to obtain the legal representation they need without facing insurmountable financial barriers.

Considerations for Clients and Law Firms

Clients should discuss payment options with their attorneys as early as possible to establish a suitable arrangement and fully understand the terms, including interest rates, payment schedules, and potential penalties. Realistically assessing their financial situation and budgeting for legal expenses can help prevent misunderstandings and financial difficulties. Law firms should be transparent about their fees and open to negotiating payment plans accommodating clients' financial situations. These plans should be documented in written agreements to prevent disputes and ensure both parties clearly understand their obligations.

Pro Se Litigant Fees

Representing yourself in a legal matter, or pro se representation, can be a daunting task involving significant financial considerations. Even without attorney fees, you must plan to spend money on various aspects of the legal process, including filing fees, court costs, subpoenas, depositions, and other related expenses (Flores, 2019):

- **Court Costs:** Besides filing fees, various court costs associated with managing and processing your case include fees for serving legal documents, court reporters, and obtaining certified copies of court records.

- **Expert Witnesses:** In some cases, especially those involving technical or specialized knowledge, you might need to hire expert witnesses. These experts can provide testimony and reports supporting your case, but their services can be expensive, sometimes costing thousands of dollars.

- **Filing Fees:** At both the trial and appellate levels, courts require filing fees for initiating lawsuits, submitting motions, and filing appeals. These fees can vary widely depending on the jurisdiction and the nature of the case. For example, filing a civil lawsuit might cost several hundred dollars, and appeals can be even more expensive.

- **Subpoenas and Depositions:** If your case involves gathering evidence or witness testimony, you may need to issue subpoenas to compel witnesses to testify or produce documents. Depositions often require payment for court reporters and transcript fees. For instance, hiring a court reporter for a deposition can cost several hundred dollars per day, and there is a per-page fee for transcripts.

By clearly presenting your case and the financial support needed, you can garner support from a broad audience, helping to alleviate the economic burden of self-representation.

Crowdfunding Your Litigation Fees

Many individuals turn to crowdfunding platforms to manage these costs and raise funds. Crowdfunding involves soliciting small contributions from many people, typically through online platforms. Here are some examples of how crowdfunding can be utilized (Coble, 2019):

- **GoFundMe:** One of the most popular crowdfunding platforms, GoFundMe allows individuals to create campaigns explaining their legal situation and the financial support they need. For example, someone facing a complex custody battle might outline their case and the anticipated costs, encouraging friends, family, and the broader community to contribute.

- **FundRazr:** Like GoFundMe, FundRazr enables users to create detailed fundraising campaigns. It supports various types of campaigns, including legal defense funds. For instance, an individual fighting a wrongful eviction could use FundRazr to cover court fees and legal expenses.

- **Kickstarter and Indiegogo:** While typically used for creative projects, these platforms can also be leveraged for personal causes, including legal battles. The success of a campaign often depends on telling a compelling story and the network of potential supporters.

- **Specialized Legal Crowdfunding Platforms:** Platforms like Funded Justice specifically focus on legal cases, providing a space for individuals to raise money for legal fees and related expenses. These platforms often attract donors who are particularly interested in supporting justice-related causes.

Representing yourself in court involves a range of financial obligations beyond just legal fees, including filing fees, court costs, subpoenas, and depositions. Utilizing crowdfunding platforms can be an effective strategy to raise the necessary funds to cover these expenses.

Kyle Rittenhouse

Kyle Rittenhouse, who faced criminal charges related to the shooting of three men during protests in Kenosha, Wisconsin, in August 2020, used crowdfunding extensively to finance his legal defense. Here are specific examples of how crowdfunding was utilized in his case (Carbonaro, 2023):

- **GiveSendGo:** Rittenhouse's supporters turned to GiveSendGo, a Christian crowdfunding platform, after being banned from mainstream sites, raising significant funds for his legal expenses by framing his case as a fight for self-defense rights.

- **FreeKyleUSA:** Supporters established the FreeKyleUSA website as a centralized hub to raise funds for Rittenhouse's defense, providing case updates, donation transparency, and direct contribution options while leveraging social media to drive donations.

- **High-Profile Endorsements:** High-profile figures and groups endorsed and financially supported Rittenhouse's case, promoting fundraising campaigns to larger audiences and significantly boosting visibility and success.

- **Legal Defense Fund Campaigns:** Various independent campaigns and events, including benefit gatherings, social media initiatives, and appeals by legal defense funds and advocacy groups, were organized to raise funds for Rittenhouse's defense, affirming his right to robust legal representation.

- **Merchandise Sales:** Fundraising efforts for Rittenhouse's defense included merchandise sales like t-shirts and hats with supportive slogans, with proceeds aiding his legal defense and fostering community among supporters.

Through these various crowdfunding efforts, Kyle Rittenhouse was able to amass substantial financial resources, enabling him to afford a comprehensive legal defense. These campaigns covered legal fees and associated costs, such as bail, expert witnesses, and trial preparation expenses. The success of these efforts underscores the significant role that crowdfunding can play in supporting individuals facing severe legal challenges.

George Zimmerman

In 2012, George Zimmerman, charged with second-degree murder in the shooting death of Trayvon Martin, extensively relied on crowdfunding to finance his legal defense. Here are specific examples of how crowdfunding was used in his case (Donations, 2012):

- **Creation of Official Defense Fund:** Zimmerman's defense team set up The George Zimmerman Defense Fund to collect donations for his legal expenses, which his attorneys managed to cover fees, court costs, and related expenses.

- **Donation Appeals During Media Interviews:** Zimmerman and his defense team utilized media appearances during the trial to appeal for donations, broadening their audience and generating additional support for his legal defense.

- **Donation Button on Legal Defense Fund Website:** The website included a prominent donation button, allowing supporters to contribute funds directly to Zimmerman's legal defense without intermediaries.

- **Personal Website:** Zimmerman's defense team launched TheRealGeorgeZimmerman.com, providing case updates, legal documents, and a donation page for supporters to contribute directly to his defense fund.

- **Support from Conservative Media Outlets:** Conservative media outlets and personalities endorsed Zimmerman, promoting his fundraising efforts and encouraging donations to his defense fund among their followers.

- **Use of Social Media Platforms:** Zimmerman's defense team used social media platforms like Facebook and Twitter to actively seek donations and promote fundraising efforts, sharing case updates and encouraging contributions to Zimmerman's defense fund.

Through these various crowdfunding efforts, George Zimmerman raised significant funds to finance his legal defense. The donations contributed to his ability to afford high-quality legal representation and cover the costs of his trial and subsequent legal proceedings. However, it's worth noting that Zimmerman's case also sparked controversy and debate surrounding the ethics of crowdfunding for individuals involved in high-profile criminal cases.

Financing protracted litigation is a complex challenge that requires careful planning and consideration of various funding options. Whether through traditional avenues like personal savings and loans or innovative approaches such as crowdfunding or grants from organizations like the American Funding Group or the Washington Lawyers' Committee for Civil Rights, individuals and organizations can find ways to access the resources needed to pursue justice through the legal system. By exploring these diverse funding sources and tailoring strategies to their specific needs, litigants can navigate the financial hurdles of protracted litigation and work toward achieving their legal objectives.

About the Author

Claudia Barber is an accomplished lawyer. She is the recipient of the 2024 Lawyers of Distinction Award. Her legal career spans 35 years. From 2005 to 2016, she served as an administrative law judge for the District of Columbia (D.C.) government. She received top performance evaluations and authored over 5,000 decisions. Many of her decisions were affirmed on appeal by the Court of Appeals for D.C.

She is a lifetime member of the National Association of Women Judges (NAWJ) and the National Bar Association. She has also previously served as president of the D.C. Association of Administrative Law Judges and as District 4 Director of NAWJ.

In 2016, she ran in a contested judicial election for the Circuit Court for Anne Arundel County. She became the first African-American woman to advance to the general election ballot. She was defeated in the general election.

Claudia Barber is also the recipient of the 2016 President's Award from the Anne Arundel County, Maryland Chapter of the NAACP, the 2022 Dr. Martin Luther King Drum Major for Justice Award, and a proud recipient of the Sojourner Truth Award from Anne Arundel County in 2022. She also served as Editor-In-Chief of the Anne Arundel County NAACP newsletter, which received the prestigious Thalmier's Award in 2022 from the National NAACP.

From 2023 to 2024, Ms. Barber served as president of the Public Sector Human Resources (PSHRA) Patuxent River Basin Chapter. In 2021, this chapter was awarded the Chapter Award of Excellence during her previous reign as IPMA Chapter President.

Claudia Barber is also an ordained Elder with her church organization, United Church of Jesus Christ, and a Sunday School Teacher and Director of Practical Living Institute.

Glossary

American Arbitration Association: A not-for-profit organization specializing in the field of alternative dispute resolution.

Arbitration: An arbitrator takes in evidence and arguments from both parties and then renders a binding decision.

Daubert Test: Set a new standard for admitting expert testimony in federal courts based on the 1993 U.S. Supreme Court case *Daubert v. Merrell Dow Pharmaceuticals, Inc.*

Ex Parte Communication: When one party in a case communicates directly with the judge without the other parties' knowledge.

Judicial Arbitration and Mediation Services: A private alternative dispute resolution provider.

Litigant: A person involved in a lawsuit.

Mediation: A mediator facilitates communication between the parties to come to an agreement.

Pro Se Litigant: A person who represents themselves in court.

Represented Litigant: A person represented by a lawyer in court.

Supreme Court: The highest court in the United States.

Surrebuttal: A rebuttal to the opposing party's rebuttal in court proceedings.

Trier of Fact: A person or group of people who decides the facts of the case—usually the jury or the judge.

Voir Dire: Third-party examination of a potential juror before selection for a jury trial.

References

About us. (n.d.). JAMS. https://www.jamsadr.com/about/

American Arbitration Association. (n.d.). *About us*. https://www.adr.org/about-us

American Bar Association. (2019, September 9). *How courts work*. ABA. https://www.americanbar.org/groups/public_education/resou rces/law_related_education_network/how_courts_work/moti onsverdict/

American Bar Association. (2021, November 28). *How courts work*. ABA. https://www.americanbar.org/groups/public_education/resou rces/law_related_education_network/how_courts_work/verdi ct/

American Bar Association. (2022, December 16). *Understanding Stare Decisis*. ABA. https://www.americanbar.org/groups/public_education/publi cations/preview_home/understand-stare-decisis/

American Bar Association. (n.d.-a). *About the ABA FJE*. ABA. https://www.americanbar.org/groups/departments_offices/FJ E/learn-about-us/

American Bar Association. (n.d.-b). *Self-represented litigants*. ABA. https://www.americanbar.org/groups/legal_aid_indigent_defe nse/resource_center_for_access_to_justice/resources--- information-on-key-atj-issues/litigant_resources/

Anastopoulo, C. A. & Cooks III, D. J. (2013). Race and gender on the bench: How best to achieve diversity in judicial selection. *Northwestern journal of law & social policy, 8(2),* 174-204.

https://scholarlycommons.law.northwestern.edu/cgi/viewcont
ent.cgi?article=1103&context=njlsp

Ash, E. & MacLeod, W. B. (2021, September). Reducing partisanship in judicial elections can improve judge quality: Evidence from U.S. state supreme courts. *Journal of public economics, 201.* https://doi.org/10.1016/j.jpubeco.2021.104478

Baldwin, J. (n.d.). *James Baldwin quotes.* GoodReads. https://www.goodreads.com/quotes/11502238-if-one-really-wishes-to-know-how-justice-is-administered

Bannon, A. (2016). Rethinking judicial selection in state courts. *Brennan Center for Justice at New York University School of Law.* https://www.brennancenter.org/sites/default/files/publication s/Rethinking_Judicial_Selection_State_Courts.pdf

Barber, C. (2021, March 16). *Voter suppression persists: Judicial reform is needed.* In City Magazine. https://incity-mag.com/voter-suppression-persists-judicial-reform-is-needed/

Bench trial. (2022, June). Cornell Law School. https://www.law.cornell.edu/wex/bench_trial

Bethune, S. (2024, February 23). *In re Robert K. Adrian Judge of the Circuit Court Eighth Judicial Circuit of the State of Illinois, respondent.* Illinois Courts Commission. https://www.illinoiscourtscommission.gov/Resources/848183 b4-119e-4184-aa72-dba12a9d2012/In%20re%20Adrian%20-%20Order%202.23.24/

Blackmun, H. A. & Supreme Court of the United States. (1992). *U.S. reports: Daubert v. Merrell Dow Pharmaceuticals, Inc. 509 U.S. 579.* [Periodical]. Library of Congress. https://www.loc.gov/item/usrep509579/

Carbonaro, G. (2023, March 3). *Kyle Rittenhouse raises $200k as supporters rush to help his legal battle.* Newsweek.

https://www.newsweek.com/kyle-rittenhouse-raises-200k-supporters-rush-help-his-legal-battle-1785284

Castaneda, R. (2016, March 31). *Former MD. judge sentenced for ordering electrical shock for defendant.* The Washington Post. https://www.washingtonpost.com/local/public-safety/former-md-judge-sentenced-for-ordering-electrical-shock-for-defendant/2016/03/31/56e31728-f752-11e5-a3ce-f06b5ba21f33_story.html

Caufield, R. P. (2010). What makes merit selection different? *Roger Williams University law review, 15(3),* 765-792. https://docs.rwu.edu/cgi/viewcontent.cgi?article=1441&context=rwu_LR

Celeste, M. A. (2010). The debate over the selection and retention of judges: How judges can ride the wave. *Court review, 46(3), 82-100.* https://digitalcommons.unl.edu/ajacourtreview/309/

Coble, C. (2019, March 21). *Should I use crowdfunding to pay for my attorney?.* FindLaw. https://www.findlaw.com/legalblogs/law-and-life/should-i-use-crowdfunding-to-pay-for-my-attorney/

Congress, House of Representatives. (2009, June 17). *H. Rept. 111-159 - Impeachment of Judge Samuel B. Kent.* https://www.congress.gov/congressional-report/111th-congress/house-report/159/1

Cook, C. (2016, May 11). *Annapolis police report differs from claims in federal lawsuit.* The Baltimore Sun. https://www.baltimoresun.com/2016/05/11/annapolis-police-report-differs-from-claims-in-federal-lawsuit/

Cooper, J. (2022, June). *Attacking and supporting witness credibility.* Advocate. https://www.advocatemagazine.com/article/2022-june/attacking-and-supporting-witness-credibility

Cooper, J. (2023, June 5). *Pro Se litigants: A word of caution*. May Oberfell Lober, LLP. https://www.maylorber.com/2023/06/05/pro-se-litigants-a-word-of-caution/

Czarnezki, J. J. (2005). A call for change: Improving judicial selection methods. *Marquette law review, 89(1), 169-178.* https://scholarship.law.marquette.edu/cgi/viewcontent.cgi?article=1092&context=mulr

Decker, S. H., Ortiz, N., Spohn, C., & Hedberg, E. (2015). Criminal stigma, race, and ethnicity: The consequences of imprisonment for employment. *Journal of criminal justice, 43, 108-121.* http://dx.doi.org/10.1016/j.jcrimjus.2015.02.002

Delete at your peril: Preserving electronic evidence during the litigation process. (2018, September 25). FindLaw. https://corporate.findlaw.com/litigation-disputes/delete-at-your-peril-preserving-electronic-evidence-during-the.html

Department of public safety and correctional services. (n.d.). *Maryland public information act.* DPSCS. https://www.dpscs.state.md.us/publicinfo/pia.shtml

District of Maryland. (2024, January 9). *USA v. Mosby, 22-cr-7.* United States District Court. https://www.mdd.uscourts.gov/news/usa-v-mosby-22-cr-7-2024-01-09t000000

District of Maryland. (2024, May 9). *Government's Sentencing Memorandum* (United States of America v. Marilyn J. Mosby 517). United States District Court. https://storage.courtlistener.com/recap/gov.uscourts.mdd.505547/gov.uscourts.mdd.505547.517.0.pdf

Donations pour in to Trayvon Martin's killer. (2012, April 26). CNN. https://www.cnn.com/2012/04/26/justice/florida-zimmerman-money/index.html

Equal justice. (n.d.). Maryland Courts. https://www.mdcourts.gov/equaljustice/committee

Felice, S. S. (2018, September 21). *Anne Arundel County's first female African-American Circuit Court judge appointed as three vacancies filled.* Capital Gazette. https://www.capitalgazette.com/2018/09/21/anne-arundel-countys-first-female-african-american-circuit-court-judge-appointed-as-three-vacancies-filled/

Find a lawyer for affordable legal aid. (2024, February 21). USA.gov. https://www.usa.gov/legal-aid

Flores, M. A. (2019, December 30). *Representing yourself can generate fees.* ABA. https://www.americanbar.org/groups/litigation/resources/litigation-news/2019/representing-yourself-can-generate-fees/

Ford Foundation. (n.d.). *Civic engagement and government.* Ford Foundation. https://www.fordfoundation.org/work/challenging-inequality/civic-engagement-and-government/

Garth, B. G., Nagel, I. H. & Plager, S. J. (1985). Empirical research and the shareholder derivative suit: Toward a better-informed debate. *Articles by Maurer Faculty, 48(3),* 137-159. https://www.repository.law.indiana.edu/cgi/viewcontent.cgi?article=2053&context=facpub

Geyh, C. G. (2014, March). The dimensions of judicial impartiality. *Florida law review, 65(2),* 493-551. https://scholarship.law.ufl.edu/cgi/viewcontent.cgi?article=1138&context=flr

Gieszl, L. & Ballou-Watts, V. (2023). *Engaging communities for equal justice.* National center for state courts. https://www.ncsc.org/__data/assets/pdf_file/0019/92161/Engaging-Communities-for-Equal-Justice.pdf

Golriz, G. S. (2023, August). *The evidence is gone...now what?* Plaintiff. https://plaintiffmagazine.com/recent-issues/item/the-evidence-is-gone-now-what

Groves, M. (2021, May 4). Judges and the media. In. G. Appleby & A. Lynch (Eds.). *The judge, the judiciary and the court: Individual, collegial and institutional judicial dynamics in Australia* (pp. 259-282). Cambridge University Press. https://www.cambridge.org/core/books/abs/judge-the-judiciary-and-the-court/judges-and-the-media/8298BBF1296918812A498E0DBB114A46

Hammond, A. (2022). The federal rules of Pro Se procedure. *Fordham Law Review, 90(6),* 2689-2775. https://ir.lawnet.fordham.edu/cgi/viewcontent.cgi?article=5947&context=flr

Harmon, N. P. (2023, August 8). *What is private arbitration?* Arbitration Agreement. https://arbitrationagreements.org/what-is-private-arbitration/

Helsel, P. (2019, September 12). *Judge recalled over Brock Turner sentence fired as girls' high school tennis coach.* NBC News. https://www.nbcnews.com/news/us-news/judge-recalled-over-brock-turner-sentence-fired-girls-high-school-n1052916

Hilotin-Lee, L. T. A. (2024, March 28). *Appealing a court decision or judgement.* FindLaw. https://www.findlaw.com/litigation/filing-a-lawsuit/appealing-a-court-decision-or-judgment.html

Holland, J. J. (2012, December 17). *Federal judges go to court over pay.* The Washington Post. https://www.washingtonpost.com/politics/federal-judges-go-to-court-over-pay/2012/12/16/d6482af6-47b2-11e2-b6f0-e851e741d196_story.html

Holland, J. J. (2013, April 22). *Court won't stop judges from getting raises.* AP. https://apnews.com/82cb2ebe9d0b4eaeb21226a9308d1dd3

Jones, N. (2021, September 17). *Caroline County Circuit Judge Newell dead after apparent suicide; faced federal complaint for alleged child sexual exploitation.* Bay Times and Record Observer. https://www.myeasternshoremd.com/qa/news/caroline-county-circuit-judge-newell-dead-after-apparent-suicide-faced-federal-complaint-for-alleged-child/article_29e0039e-e225-58a5-ad23-c377a63df279.html

Jury trial. (2023, April). Cornell Law School. https://www.law.cornell.edu/wex/jury_trial

Kang, M. S. & Shepherd, J. M. (2011, April). The partisan price of justice: An empirical analysis of campaign contributions and judicial decisions. *New York University law review, 86, 69-130.* https://www.nyulawreview.org/wp-content/uploads/2018/08/NYULawReview-86-1-Kang-Shepherd.pdf

Kurita, M. S. (2017, October). Electronic social media: Friend of foe for judges. *St. Mary's journal on legal malpractice & ethics, 7(2), 184-237.* https://commons.stmarytx.edu/cgi/viewcontent.cgi?article=1026&context=lmej

LaFleur, T. (2010, July 21). *Judge suspended for deflating tire.* NBC Washington. https://www.nbcwashington.com/news/local/judge-suspended-for-slashing-tire/1890799/

Lagratta, E. G. (2015, October). *Procedural justice: Practical tips for courts.* Center for Justice Innovation. https://www.innovatingjustice.org/sites/default/files/documents/P_J_Practical_Tips.pdf

Langs, S. J. (1997, January 1). Legal ethics — the question of *ex parte* communications and *pro se* lawyers under model rule 4.2 — hey, can we talk? *Western New England law review, 19(2), 421-453.* https://digitalcommons.law.wne.edu/cgi/viewcontent.cgi?article=1192&context=lawreview

Lederman, L. (2007, January). Disney examined: A case study in corporate governance and CEO succession. *NYLS law review, 52(4),* 557-582. https://digitalcommons.nyls.edu/nyls_law_review/vol52/iss4/5/

Legal Defense Fund. (n.d.). *History.* LDF. https://www.naacpldf.org/about-us/history/

Legal Services Corporation. (n.d.). *What is legal aid?.* LSC. https://www.lsc.gov/about-lsc/what-legal-aid

Lewis, L. (2023, September 13). *What is mediation?* FindLaw. https://www.findlaw.com/adr/mediation/what-is-mediation-.html

Livni, E. (2019, March 21). *Payment plan: Can I pay a lawyer in installments?* FindLaw. https://www.findlaw.com/legalblogs/law-and-life/payment-plan-can-i-pay-a-lawyer-in-installments/

Mangan, D. (2024, May 31). *Trump classified documents judge is target of more than 1,000 complaints, appeals court reveals.* CNBC. https://www.cnbc.com/2024/05/31/trump-classified-documents-aileen-cannon-complaints.html

Maroney, T. A. (2021). Judicial temperament, explained. *Judicature, 105(2).* https://judicature.duke.edu/articles/judicial-temperament-explained/

Maryland State Commission on Criminal Sentencing Policy. (2023, July). *An assessment of racial differences in Maryland guidelines-eligible sentencing events.* MSCCSP. https://msccsp.org/Files/Reports/Sentencing_Racial_Differences_Assessment_July2023.pdf

Maryland judiciary: Distribution of judges — race and sex. (2023, March 14). Maryland Courts. https://www.mdcourts.gov/sites/default/files/import/referen

ce/pdfs/judicialselectionworkgroup/judgesdistributionbycount
y20230314.pdf

McCleary-Evans v. Md. Dep't of Transp., 780 F.3d 582 (4th Cir. 2014).
https://casetext.com/case/mccleary-evans-v-md-dept-of-
transp-3

Merkley, J. (2014, July 9). *Merkley fights back against Hobby Lobby ruling.*
Jeff Merkley Senator for Oregon.
https://www.merkley.senate.gov/merkley-fights-back-against-
hobby-lobby-ruling/

Morris, E. S. (2021, December 29). *Daubert-proofing your expert.* ABA.
https://www.americanbar.org/groups/litigation/resources/ne
wsletters/mass-torts/daubert-proofing-your-expert/

Moser, E. (2024, March 7). *New York Times v. Sullivan: Freedom of the press
and the Civil Rights Movement.* Penn Today.
https://penntoday.upenn.edu/news/annenberg-public-policy-
new-york-times-v-sullivan-supreme-court-anniversary

Munro, D. (2023, November 29). *Maryland Gov. Wes Moore appoints judges
to Anne Arundel Circuit Court, District Court.* The Baltimore Sun.
https://www.baltimoresun.com/2023/11/29/maryland-gov-
wes-moore-appoints-judges-to-anne-arundel-circuit-court-
district-court/

Näkki, K., Mäki-Petäjä-Leinonen, A., Ervasti, K. & Solje, E. (2024,
February 16). Evaluating the need for legal guardianship in
people with dementia: Gaining insight into professionals'
assessment criteria. *International journal of law, policy, and the family,
38(1).* https://doi.org/10.1093/lawfam/ebae005

Nance, D. A. (1991). Missing evidence. *Faculty Publications, 289(13), 831-
882.* https://core.ac.uk/download/pdf/214109061.pdf

*No other individual involved in Judge Jonathan Newell's alleged exploitation of
children, images were not distributed, officials say.* (2021, December 8).
CBS News. https://www.cbsnews.com/baltimore/news/no-

other-individual-involved-in-judge-jonathan-newells-alleged-exploitation-of-children-images-were-not-distributed-officials-say/

O'Brien, R. C. (2021). Child support and joint physical custody. *Child support and joint physical custody, 70(2)*, 229-272. https://scholarship.law.edu/cgi/viewcontent.cgi?article=2035 &context=scholar

O'Neill, M. (2024, April 11). *Maryland Supreme Court grapples with rule proposals aimed at addressing systemic bias*. The Daily Record. https://thedailyrecord.com/2024/04/11/maryland-supreme-court-grapples-with-rule-proposals-aimed-at-addressing-systemic-bias/

Pandya, S. S. (2012, July 2). Unpacking the employee-misconduct defense. *Faculty articles and papers, 14(4)*, 867-925. https://digitalcommons.lib.uconn.edu/cgi/viewcontent.cgi?article=1003&context=law_papers

Raghunandan, A. (2021, June 15). Financial misconduct and employee mistreatment: Evidence from wage theft. *Review of accounting studies, 26,* 867-905. https://link.springer.com/article/10.1007/s11142-021-09602-y

The Re-invention of Billy Murphy. (n.d.). Murphy Falcon Murphy. https://www.murphyfalcon.com/firm-updates/the-re-invention-of-billy-murphy/

Reyes, J. G. (2021, March 17). *From the judge's side of the bench: The value of listening.* Decalogue Society. https://dsl.memberclicks.net/assets/docs/Tablets/Spring2021/From%20the%20Judge%E2%80%99s%20Side%20of%20the%20%20Bench-The%20Value%20of%20Listening.pdf

Robinson, J. (2023-a, August). *Daubert standard.* Cornell Law School. https://www.law.cornell.edu/wex/Daubert_standard

Robinson, J. (2023-b, August). *Verdict.* Cornell Law School. https://www.law.cornell.edu/wex/verdict

Schepard, A. (2000). The evolving judicial role in child custody disputes: From fault finder to conflict manager to differential case management. *University of Arkansas at Little Rock Law Review,* 22(3), 395-428. https://lawrepository.ualr.edu/cgi/viewcontent.cgi?referer=&httpsredir=1&article=1466&context=lawreview

Scherman, J. (2019, June 3). *20 types of evidence you may encounter as a paralegal.* Rasmussen University. https://www.rasmussen.edu/degrees/justice-studies/blog/types-of-evidence/

Sentencing subcommittee. (2021, June). Maryland Courts. https://www.mdcourts.gov/sites/default/files/import/ejc/pdf/sentencingupdate.pdf

7 types of documentary evidence you need to prove your case. (n.d.). OnRecord. https://www.myonrecord.com/blog/7-types-of-documentary-evidence-you-need-to-prove-your-case/

Smith, D. (2024, February 23). *Judge Robert Adrian removed from the bench.* WGEM. https://www.wgem.com/2024/02/23/judge-robert-adrian-removed-bench/

Sneddon, K. J. (2011). Speaking for the dead: Voice in last wills and testaments. *St. John's law review,* 85(2), 683-754. https://scholarship.law.stjohns.edu/cgi/viewcontent.cgi?referer=&httpsredir=1&article=5579&context=lawreview

Solum, L. B. & Marzen, S. J. (1989). Destruction of evidence. *Litigation, 16(1),* 11-65. http://www.jstor.org/stable/29759358

Sousou, M. (n.d.). *Robert Collier v. Dallas County Hospital: What is enough?* Harvard Undergraduate law review. https://hulr.org/spring-2021/robert-collier-v-dallas-county-hospital-what-is-enough

Spears, R. D. (2007, November). Burdens of proof. *Illinois Bar Journal, 95(11),* 604. https://www.isba.org/ibj/2007/11/burdensofproof

Supreme Court of the United States. (n.d.). *The Supreme Court at work.* Supreme Court of the United States. https://www.supremecourt.gov/about/courtatwork.aspx

Trapp, R. McLeroy, K. S., Shkolnik, N., & McCoy, R. M. (2021, September 15). *You have a judgment, now what? Mastering the art of judgment collection.* ABA. https://www.americanbar.org/groups/business_law/resources/business-law-today/2021-september/you-have-a-judgment/

Tuskai, J. E. (2021, November 12). *Judicial selection in the United States: An overview.* ABA. https://www.americanbar.org/groups/judicial/publications/judges_journal/2021/fall/judicial-selection-the-united-states-overview/

United States courts. (n.d.). *Supreme Court procedures.* United States courts. https://www.uscourts.gov/about-federal-courts/educational-resources/about-educational-outreach/activity-resources/supreme-1

U.S. Merit Systems Protection Board. (2019, October). *Judges' handbook.* MSPB. https://www.mspb.gov/appeals/files/ALJHandbook.pdf

Vogeler, W. (2019, June 3). *If you didn't know, family law can kill you.* FindLaw. https://www.findlaw.com/legalblogs/strategist/if-you-didnt-know-family-law-can-kill-you/

Ware, S. J. (2022, April 25). Judicial selection that fails the separation of powers. *Catholic University law review, 72,* 299. https://dx.doi.org/10.2139/ssrn.4093255

Washington Lawyers' Committee. (n.d.). *About us.* Washington Lawyers' Committee. https://www.washlaw.org/about-us/

Waxman, O. B. (2021, March 30). *How a 1946 case of police brutality against a black WWII veteran shaped the fight for Civil Rights*. Time. https://time.com/5950641/blinding-isaac-woodard/

Weathers, B. (2016, April 19). *Judicial challenger accuses sitting judge of misrepresenting her experience*. Capital Gazette. https://www.capitalgazette.com/2016/04/19/judicial-challenger-accuses-sitting-judge-of-misrepresenting-her-experience/

Weiner, I. (2021, May 12). *Maryland judge signs off on landmark settlement of HBCU litigation, ending 15-year case*. Lawyers' committee for civil rights. https://www.lawyerscommittee.org/maryland-judge-signs-off-on-landmark-settlement-of-hbcu-litigation-ending-15-year-case/

What is a Motion for Reconsideration? (2021, September 21). WomensLaw.org. https://www.womenslaw.org/laws/preparing-court-yourself/after-decision-issued/motions-reconsideration/what-motion

Williams, S. (2023, October 3). *Appeals, appellate courts, and costs*. FindLaw. https://www.findlaw.com/criminal/criminal-procedure/appeals-appellate-courts-and-costs.html

Williams, S. (2024, January 3). *Evidence: The concept of 'admissibility.'* FindLaw. https://www.findlaw.com/criminal/criminal-procedure/evidence-the-concept-of-admissibility.html

www.ingramcontent.com/pod-product-compliance
Lightning Source LLC
Chambersburg PA
CBHW060236030426
42335CB00014B/1476